FINANCIAL PLANNING & YOU

Financial Planning & You

Smart Strategies for 5 Crucial Chapters of Your Retirement Journey

ADRIAN ALBIDRESS, JR.
CFP® CPA

ALBIDRESS
—FINANCIAL—

To my wife Sara, daughters Ava & Emily, my parents Adrian and Sylvia Albidress, and all my family, friends, and clients who have supported me on my journey.

PREFACE

With knowledge that I've accumulated working as a Certified Financial Planner® and Certified Public Accountant, I hope to help you embrace each chapter of your life skillfully and confidently. I've had thousands of conversations with clients and colleagues alike and I hope to pass on some of the things I've learned to you.

You can learn more about me and my work at www.financialplanningandyou.com and www.albidressfinancial.com. Albidress Financial is an asset management firm dedicated to helping people pursue their financial goals with clarity and confidence. We serve clients locally in the Maryland/Delaware/Pennsylvania tri-state area as well as remotely in other states across the country. We also enjoy involving ourselves in the community with interactive teaching workshops and speaking engagements. To inquire about our services, workshops, speaking engagements, or any other questions you may have, please reach out to me at a.albidress@lpl.com.

Thank you for reading this book, I wish you success on your journey!

-Adrian Albidress, Jr. CFP® CPA

TABLE OF CONTENTS

Long-term Care Funding
Fraud & Liability Protection
Losing Loved Ones
Executor Checklist
Opportunities Lie Ahead

Accredited Investors
Asset Protection
Roth Conversion
Concentrated Portfolios
Estate Tax
Gifting Strategies
Personal Property & Real Property
Joint Ownership & Community Property
Life Estate
Trusts
Embracing Success

Naming a Fiduciary
Probate
Step-up in Basis Vs. Gifting Assets
Inherited IRAs
Trusts as Beneficiaries
Estate Liquidity
Death Benefit Riders
Business Succession Planning
Philanthropy & Charitable Tax Savings Strategies
Cognitive Decline & Death
Leadership & Legacy

INTRODUCTION

Financial planning is the foundation of your greater journey. Working as a Certified Financial Planner® and Certified Public Accountant, I have had the opportunity to learn and grow from thousands of conversations with my clients. Hearing my client's life stories has taught me numerous valuable lessons. What lessons would others learn if they knew your story?

To best capture the imaginations of readers, stories tend to follow certain templates. The most common template identified in comparative mythology and narratology is sometimes referred to as the Hero's Journey. The Hero's Journey involves an archetypal hero seeking adventure, emerging victorious against powerful forces, and eventually coming back home transformed. This hero archetype can be found in stories throughout history and all around the world, from modern day Hollywood to long before the written word was even common. If your life story were to be made into a movie, the Hero's Journey is the template for the script.

What insights can be gained if you observe your life objectively from the perspective of an unbiased storyteller? This book will motivate clearer thinking, healthier financial decision making, and discuss a variety of financial topics and strategies that will aid you in your retirement journey. For the hero to prevail in real life, a certain amount of money is necessary. While money can't buy happiness, it can provide a foundation. From this foundation, life's inevitable challenges can be faced from a position of security and strength. In this book, we will frame the Hero's Journey narrative through the lens of financial planning in retirement. We will learn how to master the financial forces at work in 5 crucial chapters of your retirement journey.

Think of yourself as the central character of your own story. Using the familiar patterns of traditional storytelling will help us anticipate the chapters of your life story as they unfold. With knowledge that I've accumulated working as a Certified Financial Planner® and Certified Public Accountant, I hope to help you embrace each chapter of your life skillfully and confidently. When it comes to matters like estate planning and investment portfolio rebalancing, it is easy to get complacent. My expectation is that greater clarity will motivate you to take proactive steps to better your financial future. In this book, we will look at a variety of tools and strategies to accomplish your financial goals. By the end of this book, you will have a clearer vision of yourself at the end of your journey. What do you want to accomplish in the next ten years? What steps do you need to take now to put you in the financial position you want to be in? If you're dead, does it even matter? These are all good questions. To answer these questions, it helps to take a step back from your daily habits and comfort zone. Storytelling allows us to see ourselves with a fresh set of eyes.

Retirement isn't the end of your journey. Your story is only beginning!

| 1 |

PRE-RETIREMENT PLANNING

People come from an amazingly wide variety of economic backgrounds and therefore have a diversity of beliefs regarding the subject of money. Think back to your childhood. How was money discussed in your household? How did your financial situation contrast with that of your peer group? Is it a necessary evil? A useful tool? Is more always better? For some, the journey towards financial success requires a radical rethinking of wealth. Not everyone receives a solid financial education. We've all heard stories about former athletes and lottery winners losing their money to unfortunate decisions and bad investments. Everyone wants to enjoy money, but even the affluent must be disciplined and know their limits. Achieving goals requires you to take a hard look at your financial habits and attitudes. What does wealth mean to you? What benefits does wealth have to offer?

As your retirement journey beings, much of your future success hinges on your ability to establish and maintain good financial habits. If your habits need improvement, don't judge yourself too harshly. You don't need to transform yourself into a hyper-rational economic machine either. If you can somehow manage to take financial decision making seriously without taking yourself too seriously, you've made a great accomplishment! To establish a healthy financial comfort zone, you need to master the 9 good habits of personal finance.

9 GOOD HABITS OF PERSONAL FINANCE

A common plot device in movies and television is the training montage. In the span of only a few minutes, we see a character like Rocky Balboa mold themselves into a rejuvenated, stronger version of themselves. In real life we don't get to remake ourselves that quickly. Lasting greatness takes time and requires us to form and adhere to good habits. Which of your habits have helped you on your journey thus far? Which habits have caused suffering? Habit formation is a marathon, not a sprint. Forming good habits may not always feel fun, but good habits ultimately make life more satisfying to experience.

Everyone's journey is different, and everyone has unique strengths, weaknesses, challenges, and opportunities. In general, however, it is safe to say you should always try to establish these 9 universal good financial habits:

1. Earn more than you spend until you've built a sustainable nest egg.
2. Establish an emergency fund.
3. Pay bills on time.
4. Be mindful of what you buy. What purpose do your purchases serve?
5. Reduce or eliminate high-interest debt.
6. Set your own financial standards. It isn't fair to yourself to compare yourself to others.
7. Use money to acquire growth and income-producing assets.

8. Understand your investment risk tolerance and time horizon.
9. Set goals and monitor your progress.

People aren't perfect, me included. I can, however, share financial strategies with you that will help on your journey. In working with my clients, I help them proactively establish good habits like organization, accountability, investment monitoring, and education on relevant emerging financial topics. Clearly understanding your finances will allow you to make better life decisions. If you need help addressing any personal challenges affecting your ability to successfully pursue your financial goals, please reach out to someone who is qualified to help you. Remember that your financial habits are affected by your non-financial habits. Addressing a bad habit is a sign of strength, not an acknowledgement of weakness.

YOUR INNER FINANCIAL CIRCLE

A hero doesn't journey alone. Americans may be known for rugged individualism, but there is a limit to what one person can accomplish. Most stories include one or more characters that serve as a hero's guide, like Yoda from Star Wars or Gandalf from the Lord of the Rings. These guides will often have magical or mysterious powers.

I don't know magic, but I am familiar with many of the challenges retirees will face and how to anticipate and address their challenges. One of your most important tasks is to establish your own personal circle of influence. Those within this circle may be friends, family, and qualified professionals. A great guide should be able to help you with the following:

-Organization
-Education

-Clarity
-Accountability
-Objectivity
-Proactivity
-Confidence

Trust and competence are critical factors to consider when letting someone into your inner financial circle and conflicts of interest must be managed and accounted for. Ideally, your inner circle will be experienced, understand what your financial goals are, and understand why and how you want to achieve them. They should empower you to live a happier and more productive life. Your inner circle is one of your most important assets. With grit, determination, and multiple coffee refills there are a lot of things you can accomplish on your own. How much do you want to do on your own? If you spend all your time solving problems, will you have time left to discover new opportunities? Remember to value the opportunity costs and precious wasted time of trying to do everything by yourself.

PERSONAL FINANCIAL STATEMENTS

Financial statements are most often thought of in a business context, but they are crucial tools for individuals too. How else would you get a clear picture of your financial standing? Generally, it is to your advantage to acquire a variety of assets and establish multiple streams of income. Acquiring assets and diverse revenue sources creates a good problem: tracking and monitoring your financial position.

A common phrase in many professional fields is the term "garbage in, garbage out." To create useful statements, you need to make sure you are using reliable data inputs. A concept to consider is materiality. In an accounting context, materiality is defined as a subjective measurement used to judge misstatements in financial reporting. Put bluntly, if something is material, it is worth tracking and monitoring. If a misstatement is material, this means that the misstatement could reasonably be expected to influence the economic decision making of the financial statement user. If something is immaterial, the misstatement isn't profound enough to have that same affect. As a user of your own personal financial statements, you are the ultimate judge of whether something is material or immaterial. The two most important financial statements for you to familiarize yourself with are the Statement of Net Worth and the Net Income Statement. Creating positive net income is the key to building net worth.

STATEMENT OF NET WORTH

The statement of net worth is a great tool for measuring your financial position. It may also be referred to as a statement of financial position or a personal balance sheet. Net worth is calculated by subtracting your total liabilities from the total value of your assets. An asset is property that has value and can be used to pay expenses or be passed on to others. An asset may be tangible, like a car or piece of artwork, or intangible like a patent or copyright. Some assets, like stocks and bonds, are considered liquid, meaning that they can be bought and sold with relative ease and timeliness. Assets that may be more difficult to sell, like real estate or rare collectibles, are considered illiquid. Liabilities are financial commitments that must be paid within a specified time frame. When adding up your assets, remember to consider materiality. It isn't realistic or practical to add up every single thing that you own!

EXAMPLE: PERSONAL STATEMENT OF NET WORTH

Jane Smith
Personal Statement of Net Worth
July 4, 20XX

Assets	Estimated Value
Car	$ 30,000
Home	$ 350,000
Cash	$ 50,000
401(k)	$ 500,000
Brokerage	$ 120,000
Total Assets	**$ 1,050,000**
Liabilities	**Estimated Value**
Car Loan	$ 18,000
Mortgage	$ 110,000
Total Liabilities	**$ 128,000**
Net Worth	**$ 922,000**

NET INCOME STATEMENT

Net worth doesn't magically appear to us. Even if you inherit money, that money came from some combination of hard work, opportunity, and risk taking. Most of us will need net income to build net worth. Net income is calculated by subtracting total expenses from total revenue over a given timeframe. Due to the variable nature of income and expenses, it can feel difficult gauging how you are doing financially. Some months you may feel like are doing well, and other months you may feel you are falling behind. The net income statement is a great tool for measuring how much income you will have available to reinvest.

Ultimately, you need income to exceed expenses so you can establish an emergency fund and put your remaining earnings to work. The more money you can put to work, the greater your net worth will grow. As you analyze your net worth statement, ask yourself; "What can I do to increase my net revenue?" This might mean increasing your income, reducing your spending, or both.

A concept related to net income is cash flow. When it comes to earning and spending money, timing is critical, and you need to make sure cash is available to meet short term obligations. Positive cash flows generally indicate that you are doing a good job making money and negative cash flows might be a warning sign that you are overspending. Temporary negative cash flows may not be a bad thing if your cash outflows are funding activity that generates future growth (i.e. investments). Financing may bring cash inflows in the near term, but if the funds are not used wisely then future debt service expenses may hurt more than the original cash inflow helped. Always consider cash flow in unison with your statement of net worth and net income.

EXAMPLE: PERSONAL NET INCOME STATEMENT

Jane Smith
Personal Net Income Statement
January 1, 20XX – December 31, 20XX

Income		
Wage Income	$	155,000
Capital Gains	$	5,300
Interest Income	$	400
Total Income	**$**	**160,700**
Expenses		
Rent	$	36,000
Utilities	$	2,400
Vehicle Expenses	$	9,200
Food	$	8,100
Entertainment	$	7,900
Insurance	$	6,800
Taxes	$	40,100
Total Expenses	**$**	**110,500**
Total Net Income	**$**	**50,200**

RETIREMENT NEEDS ANALYSIS

How much money do you need to retire? This is the question that leads millions to seek professional financial advice. Given the uncertainty of powerful variables like market risk, inflation, and life expectancy, it is a difficult question to answer. How do we gain a greater degree of clarity? A key component of formal financial plans is the retirement needs analysis. This analysis is typically conducted with specialized financial software and is intended to produce a reasonable estimate of how your long your money will last in retirement. There are 10 relevant assumptions to consider:

1. How much time you have until you retire
2. Your investment risk tolerance
3. Your retirement income sources (social security, pensions, annuities, etc.)
4. When you need to start accessing your retirement income sources (time horizon)
5. Your life expectancy
6. Expenses (including both recurring expenses and anticipated large, one-time purchases)
7. Assets (IRA's, Retirement Plans, Brokerage Accounts, etc.)
8. Liabilities (Mortgage, Credit Cards, etc.)
9. An assumed rate of return on your investments
10. An assumed inflation rate on your expenses

A retirement needs analysis is useful to project how much money you will have in the future given these assumptions. The longer you continue working, the more likely it is that you won't outlive your money. Depending on who you are, working for longer may sound fine to you. Many of us, however, are eager to retire but fear that doing so too soon will create unacceptable financial risk. Even if you don't intend to retire soon, it is important to know where you stand financially. Ideally, you will set the timeline for your own retirement, but sometimes circumstances force your hand. Hope for the best, but plan for the worst. Not everyone gets the luxury of choosing their own destiny.

A needs analysis may tell you that you need to work longer to afford your current lifestyle for the duration of your life expectancy. While this may not be the news you are hoping for, you will at least be able to set tangible goals. An obvious choice would be to work longer. You might also be able to continue working part time or at a new job that pays less but is more enjoyable. Employment can be a fantastic part of your journey if you are doing something you enjoy.

When considering life expectancy, please remember that people are living longer than ever before. Wonderful advancements are being made in the early prevention and treatment of cancer and other illnesses. This is a great thing, but it introduces more people to the threat of outliving their assets. When doing a needs analysis, try modeling scenarios where you live longer than you expect to.

When analyzing your retirement income sources and expenses, more accurate inputs will give you more reliable results. The further into the future you project, the harder it is to be accurate. Your analysis must consider the high variability of outcomes for risk factors like stock performance and inflation. It is important to consider a wide range of scenarios. Small tweaks- even an adjustment of a half-percent- can make a difference of years to you in terms of your ability to afford retirement. It is wise to consult with a qualified financial advisor who can help you develop and interpret the results of your analysis.

An analysis might be conducted assuming that your capital is depleted over your life expectancy. If your goal is die having spent every penny, this should suit you well. However, this begs the question: When will you die? What happens if you live longer than you can afford to? With this in mind, you might model scenarios in which you draw income from your assets but keep your principal intact. You can take this thought one step further by using an inflation-adjusted interest rate to not only preserve your original principal, but have it increase as needed to account for inflation.

When settings goals, you may find it helpful to categorize them into the following categories: must have, want to have, and great to have. When it comes to expenses, it is important to consider how your spending is likely to evolve throughout your retirement. New retirees pursue a variety of activities like hobbies, travel, and more. In time, it is natural for us to slow down. As we slow down, we are less likely to be spending money on big ticket items. At the same time, health care expenses and other retirement-centric spending may increase as you age.

Since we do not know exactly what the future holds, we must anticipate a range of possibilities. With so many possibilities, how can we get a clearer sense of the future? As part of a needs analysis, many advisors use a tool called a Monte Carlo simulation to predict the probability of different outcomes given different variables like life expectancy, rate of return, market volatility, and inflation. The Monte Carlo simulation helps predict in percentage terms what your odds are of reaching a specific financial goal. Within the needs analysis, you can tweak aspects of you financial planning data inputs to reflect possible behavioral changes that will help increase your percentage chances of achieving a financial goal. For example, you can estimate in percentage terms how working an extra 2 years at your current job may help your money last the duration of your life-time. You may find working another year or two makes a dramatic difference in your outlook.

IRAS AND EMPLOYER-SPONSORED RETIREMENT PLANS

For many Americans, their retirement account is their largest asset. These assets are a foundational piece in funding your journey. Defined benefit, defined contribution, IRA, 401(k), 403(b), etc.- the number of retirement plan categories out there is enough to confuse both amateurs and professionals alike. What do they all have in common? All profit-sharing & tax-advantaged plans offer an incentive to make contributions to an account that is earmarked for future retirement spending. For participants aged 50 and over, catch-up contributions are allowed to help stash away extra money in what are often an individual's peak earning years.

Individual retirement accounts (IRAs) and employer-sponsored plans have many similarities, but they all have their own rules which we will discuss throughout this book. A key differentiator is that IRAs are owned by you alone with no strings attached to an un-related employer. Employer-sponsored plans generally have higher tax-advantaged contribution limits than IRAs. IRAs may serve as a supplement to an employer-sponsored plan, but active participation in an employer-sponsored may preclude you from deducting your IRA contribution if your income exceeds certain thresholds. How can you find out if you are eligible for an IRA? Contact a qualified advisor, check out the IRS website, or visit www.albidressfinan-cial.com/learning_center/calculators, and scroll down until you see the IRA eligibility tool.

Much has been said about the demise of traditional pensions. While the defined-benefit pension has become less common, the defined contribution plan has become the norm. Business can be volatile, and many business owners are understandably reluctant to commit to the mandatory annual funding required of defined benefit pensions. In a defined contribution plan, the employer makes a formula-based contribution to each employee participant.

Employers have more flexibility with a defined contribution plan in that they can make contributions at their discretion instead of making the annual mandatory contributions required by a defined benefit plan. Participants have their own individual account and choose their own investments. The investment risk is shifted from the employer to the employee. A defined contribution plan may take the form of one of several types of profit-sharing plan: 401(k)'s, SIMPLE 401(k)'s, age-based plans, stock bonus plans, employee stock ownership plans, and thrift plans. Profit sharing plans do not provide a specific benefit like a pension plan does and employers are not required to fund them annually. Unlike a pension, a profit-sharing plan can include greater than 10% of the employer's own securities- even as much as 100%. New employer-sponsored qualified plans may receive tax credits to help offset start-up costs.

The name "profit-sharing" plan implies you are a part of a company that makes a profit. What about plans for nonprofit organizations? A variety of plans exist that function similar to profit-sharing plans: 403(b)s, 457s, tax-sheltered annuities, and thrift savings plans. These plans are common with nonprofit organizations, governments, and public educational institutions.

The self-employed also can consider simplified employee pension (SEP) IRAs and savings incentive match plans for employees (SIMPLE). The SEP IRA is a type of IRA that is popular with sole practitioners and employers that would like to make flexible, discretionary contributions to their employees. A SEP IRA is cheaper and easier to administer than a qualified profit-sharing plan. Employer contributions must be made on a nondiscriminatory basis and employees can roll over their SEP IRA accounts to their own traditional IRA in the future if desired. The SIMPLE plan can be either an IRA or 401(k) and is available to employers with 100 or less employees. If you are self-employed, be sure to do your research or speak with a qualified advisor to set up a plan that best fits your needs.

As you can see, there are a plethora of plans. With so many choices, how does an employer choose which plan or combination of plans to go with? There are two questions employers can ask themselves to help decide: 1) Do you want this plan to help attract, retain, and incentivize employees? 2) Do you want the plan to favor the business owner(s) or certain age groups? It is common for employers to choose a plan that maximizes a retirement benefit for themselves or a small group. If the employer or an intended group of key employees skews older than the other employers, an age-based profit-sharing plan might be appropriate. For employers focused on growing their business, traditional profit-sharing plans, employee stock option plans, and employee stock bonus plans might be a great way to align your employee's personal financial goals with your own. Employers must factor in the cost to administer a plan and the responsibilities a plan entails.

If you are a business owner, how do feel about nondiscrimination rules in your company's plan? Employers must adhere to various nondiscrimination testing protocols to ensure that their qualified plan isn't favoring highly compensated employees. If this is untenable, a nonqualified plan may be a better choice. What's the difference between qualified and nonqualified plans? Nonqualified plans do not have all the benefits of qualified and tax-advantaged plans, but they are not subject to all the same discrimination rules either. For this reason, they are often used with highly compensated employees to supplement qualified plan benefits.

ROTH

How do you feel about tax-free earnings? Traditional tax-advantaged accounts and their Roth counterparts both offer tax advantages. The difference is in timing. The traditional tax-advantaged account gives you a tax benefit up front. Eventually, when you pull the money out, it is taxable to the extent your contributions were made with pretax dollars. Roth accounts give you the tax benefit on the back end. They are funded with after-tax contributions, but the earnings aren't taxable if you meet the basic qualified distribution requirements. Contributions can be pulled out penalty free if desired at any time. A qualified Roth distribution can only occur after a 5-year holding period and when one of the following criteria is met:

- The owner attains the age of 59.5
- The owner becomes disabled
- A distribution is made to a beneficiary or estate after the owner's death

If you have are a high earner, income limits may preclude you from making contributions directly to a Roth IRA. There is a work around available, however- at least for the time being. The "backdoor" Roth is a tactic involving a nondeductible contribution to a traditional IRA followed up with a conversion to a Roth IRA. While there are income limits for contributing to a Roth IRA, there are no such limits for converting a traditional IRA to a Roth IRA. This is useful for taxpayers who earn too much to make a Roth contribution directly. Some employer-sponsored plans even offer the ability to make a "mega" backdoor Roth contribution, which is like the regular backdoor Roth but with higher contribution limits. This is only allowed in certain plans that allow after-tax contributions and in-service distributions. Discuss this strategy with both your tax advisor and human resource department before implementing! Lawmakers have discussed the elimination of the back door Roth in the past, but for now it remains a useful tool. If you have traditional IRAs with both deductible and nondeductible contributions, remember to aggregate their value when calculating the taxable portion of the conversion.

When converting an IRA that is funded with 100% deductible contributions, the entirety of the converted amount is taxable income. When converting an IRA that was funded with nondeductible contributions, a portion of the conversion is a nontaxable return of basis. What if you have some money in deductible IRAs and other money in nondeductible IRAs? Can you convert only the nondeductible IRA to reap the benefits of a Roth conversion while minimizing current taxation? There are rules in places to prevent taxpayers from doing this. Even if you keep your deductible and nondeductible IRAs in separate accounts, they must be aggregated when determining the portion of your conversion that is taxable. The end result is that the amount of a Roth conversion that is free of tax is proportional to the amount of basis in the IRAs.

I am often asked if Roth IRAs are better than traditional IRAs. The answer isn't crystal clear because we do not know what tax rates will be in the future. On one hand, I never see people upset about tax free money in retirement. However, if you are in a low tax bracket in retirement, the upfront tax benefit of a traditional IRA may have helped you more in the past then the Roth helps you in the present or future. Additionally, there are rules that could change in the future. For example, there are no required minimum distributions from a Roth account during the owner's lifetime under today's tax rules. This is a nice feature if you want to keep your investments growing tax free beyond your early 70's or potentially pass assets to your heirs tax-free. Law changes are part of what makes my job interesting, challenging, and sometimes frustrating.

If you own investments or other appreciable assets outside of a retirement plan, it is important to know the tax implications. The rules can be quite nuanced, so it is wise to discuss your holdings with a qualified tax advisor. When you sell appreciated assets, you realize a capital gain. Assets held longer than a year qualify for preferential long-term capital gains rates.

While the majority of many people's investments are in their qualified retirement plans, there are some unique benefits and strategies available to assets held in taxable accounts. We will discuss some of these strategies throughout the book.

PENSIONS

"Why don't companies offer pensions anymore?" I am sometimes asked. Pensions are becoming more and more rare, particularly in the private sector. This can be a complex subject, but a big part of it has to do with the costly actuarial work and mandatory funding rules required of a pension plan. Funding a reliable guarantee is not cheap or easy.

If you do have a pension, it is useful to know what kind of pension you have. If you are a business owner, it is wise to familiarize yourself with the options available to you. In simple terms, a pension is a promise from the employer to pay a specific retirement benefit to a plan participant in the future. Pensions offer protection for the pensioners spouses in the form of preretirement survivor annuities (if the plan participant dies before retiring) and joint and survivor annuities. No one retirement plan is best for every business, and each option has tradeoffs that the business owner needs to discuss with a qualified advisor. Types of pension plans include:

- Traditional defined benefit pensions
- DB(k) pension plans
- Cash balance pensions
- Money purchase pensions
- Target benefit pensions

An employer-sponsored qualified retirement plan can take the form of either a pension or a profit-sharing plan. With a defined-benefit pension, the investment risk falls on the employer and investments are held in a commingled account. The employer receives a tax deduction when they make contributions, and the employee is not taxed until they take distributions from the pension in the future. Benefits are determined based on a formula considering a retiring employees age and length of service.

A less common variant of the defined plan is the DB(k) plan. It is a type of defined benefit pension that functions as a hybrid between a typical defined benefit pension and a 401(k). This type of plan can accept pretax employee contributions. For smaller employers, this may be a way to establish a defined benefit plan with lower costs.

A cash balance plan is another type of pension plan that mimics some features of a defined contribution plan. Most cash balance plans started as defined benefit plans and were later converted. They are more likely to be used by a larger employer (where administrative costs can be spread amongst many employees) and are less likely to favor older participants. Generally, they are less expensive than traditional defined benefit plans and more costly than defined contribution plans. In a cash balance plan, employers make contributions to each participant with an employer-guaranteed rate of return. Contributions to a cash balance plan are made based on a percentage of salary instead of an actuarial calculation.

A common fear for pensioners is that their defined-benefit pension plan provider will become insolvent in the future and fail to fulfill their financial promises. Who wants to work loyally for decades only to see their benefits disappear in retirement? While this technically is a possibility, there are a few measures in place to mitigate this risk. A defined-benefit pension is limited to 10% employer securities, which gives a measure of protection in case the employer's shares declined. Also, defined benefit plans must be funded annually and are subject to mandatory insurance coverage under the Pension Benefit Guarantee Corporation (PBGC). If a distressed defined benefit plan must be terminated, the PBGC will be liable for at least a portion of the balance. Some plans may be fully funded and guaranteed by an insurance company using cash value life insurance or an annuity contract.

A defined-contribution pension is an alternative to the defined-benefit pension plan in which the employer must still make annual contributions, but the employee takes the investment risk instead. Compared to defined benefit plans, defined contribution plans are relatively simple and affordable. Unlike defined benefit plans and cash balance plans, defined contribution plans are not insured by the PBGC. Like a defined benefit plan, the number of years in service will affect how much benefit a participant will accrue. Contributions are deductible to the employer at the time of contribution and taxable upon distribution in the future.

A target benefit pension is a hybrid between a defined benefit plan and defined contribution pension plan. It aims to create a specific retirement income benefit like a defined benefit plan does while shifting the risk to the participant instead of the employer. While there are still nondiscrimination rules to follow, a target benefit pension can be age-weighted to favor older participants. These plans can be a lower cost alternative to a defined benefit plan, although they still require mandatory annual funding. Target benefit pensions are not covered by PBGC and an actuary is needed when a plan is established.

How about a pension plan that doesn't need costly actuarial services? The money purchase pension plan is a type of qualified defined contribution plan where employers make mandatory, annual payments to each employee's account. The amount of the contribution is based on a nondiscriminatory formula and may be more favorable to younger employees than other plans. When an employee separates from service, they may take a distribution from the plan as either a lump sum, rollover, or an annuity payment. Some plans may allow after-tax employee contributions. If your business has young employees and your goal is to optimize tax-advantaged planning for yourself and/or older employees, there might be better plans to meet your goals. Traditional profit-sharing plans are often preferred to money purchase pension plans because they do not require annual funding.

"Are any businesses even creating new pension plans?" you might wonder. They're not as common, but pensions can be appealing near an employer's retirement because of the large amounts of tax-advantaged contributions that can be made.

STOCK BONUS PLANS & EMPLOYEE STOCK OPTION PLANS

Stock bonus plans differ from other profit-sharing plans in that participants receive benefits in the form of company stock. If you own stock from a company whose shares are not easily tradable, your plan might allow you to request that your employer repurchase shares at a fair price. Stock bonus plans can be a great incentive for employees, but they can also lead to concentrated portfolios. From an employer's perspective, stock plans may give employees more control than the employer is comfortable with in the form of voting rights. This could potentially factor into executive decisions like mergers and liquidations.

A variant of the stock bonus plan is the employee stock ownership plan (ESOP). A well-executed ESOP can be a cost-effective way for an incorporated business to transfer company stock to its employees. ESOPs differ from stock bonus plans in that they may function as a way for the employer to receive favorable lending terms. First, a financial institution lends money to a third-party ESOP trustee. The ESOP trustee then uses the loan proceeds to purchase the employer stock from the corporate shareholders. The employer then makes tax deductible contributions to the ESOP to pay off the loan. Does that sound complicated? An ESOP is worth the effort for incorporated businesses that can A) use the tax deduction, B) benefit from establishing a market for their shares, and C) capitalize on borrowing opportunities. A shareholder that reinvests ESOP proceeds into domestic securities receives beneficial tax treatment if certain rules are met, creating an opportunity to diversify without negative tax consequences.

A unique feature of stock bonus plans and ESOPs is the opportunity to take advantage of special tax rules regarding net unrealized appreciation. "What is net unrealized appreciation?" you might ask. Net unrealized appreciation is the difference between the stock's fair market value and its tax basis. If you take a lump sum distribution of employer stock, you can elect to recognize the ordinary income on the transaction equal to the value of the stock at the time of contribution to the plan. What is the benefit to doing so? The benefit is that the net unrealized appreciation will be treated as a capital gain instead of ordinary income when the stock is sold in the future. As we've discussed, long term capital gains are given preferential tax treatment.

ASSET CLASSES

It has been said that a blindfolded monkey throwing darts at the financial newspaper pages can pick stocks as well as a stock market expert. Can you build an investment portfolio smarter than a blindfolded monkey? In attempting to do so, there are two metrics that I consider: winning percentage and margin of victory. In 1989, the San Francisco 49ers beat the Cincinnati Bengals in Super Bowl XXIII by a margin of 4 points. The very next year, they won Super

Bowl XXIV against the Denver Broncos by a margin of 45 points. Did the margin of victory make one Super Bowl win better than the other? A personal quirk of mine is that I frequently think of life in terms of football metaphors. Stocks are like the passing game that puts most of your points on the scoreboard and bonds are like the running game that helps secure victory once you've established a comfortable margin. When it comes to your journey, how do you define victory? How close are you right now to achieving it?

A 2017 study by the Vanguard group found that 91% of portfolio performance was the result of asset class selection and only 9% was a matter of security selection and market timing (Scott, Brian J., James Balsamo, Kelly N. McShane and Christos Tasopoulos, 2017. The Global Case for Strategic Asset Allocation and an Examination of Home Bias. Valley Forge, Pa.: The Vanguard Group). To the extent that portfolio performance is a result of stock picking and market timing, it is hard to beat the blindfolded monkey. Where investors have more control is in their choice of asset classes. One of my favorite tools for discussing asset classes is the risk pyramid.

A risk pyramid is a simple visual tool that orders different asset classes in terms of risk. At the base of a risk pyramid is a foundation composed of relatively safe assets like cash and U.S. Treasuries. At the top of the pyramid are the riskiest assets like emerging market stocks and commodities. In between the top and the base are a variety of asset classes with their own risk/reward proposition, ranked by safety from bottom to top. The perfect theoretical investment is easy to purchase, simple to understand, has a high rate of return, is completely safe, is fully liquid, and is tax-free. Since such an investment doesn't exist, an investor needs to make certain tradeoffs. Typically, when you are in the early stages of your career and you have many years to save for retirement, your retirement assets will have an aggressive allocation with more exposure to the higher risk assets at the top of the pyramid. As you get closer to retirement, more consideration needs to be given to asset classes in the lower and middle levels.

INVESTMENT RISK PYRAMID

As an advisor, I have always liked the concept of the risk pyramid. It is a simple, clear image that is great for communicating the basic idea of asset class risks to clients. If an asset lies closer to the foundational layer, we might assume it has little upside, but this isn't entirely true. Is the risk/reward proposition static? The relative risk/reward proposition of certain financial products like annuities and structured bank notes changes in different interest rate environments. When interest rates are higher, the banks and insurance companies offering these products are usually able to make more compelling offers to consumers. How do low interest rate environments affect financial institutions like banks and insurance companies? When interest rates are low, it might be harder for a financial institution to be profitable. Imagine trying to make money as a lender when everyone with decent credit is paying you close to zero percent interest.

The sheer number of asset classes and investment choices can be overwhelming. Some of these choices are complex and expensive. Let's take a closer look at some of the different assets you can find in the risk pyramid and discuss how they might serve you along your journey.

STOCKS

When you own publicly traded stock, you own a small piece of a large corporation. A great starting point for understanding stocks is the Morningstar style box.

Looking horizontally on the style box, we have value stocks on the left, growth stocks on the right, and core stocks in the middle. What's the difference between value, growth, and core? Value stocks are typically characterized by metrics like higher-than-average dividend yields and relatively low price to earnings ratios. Value investors look to see if the stock is "on sale", meaning that it's underpriced relative to what the stocks true value is. Growth style investors tend to look for companies with higher-than-average growth rates. A growth company might have little profit in the short term and pay little to no dividend. Why would one purchase stock in a company that is not profitable? The expectation is that the investor is getting in early on a company with a bright future.

Vertically on the style box, we have large-cap stocks on top, mid-cap stocks in the middle, and small-cap stocks on the bottom. Large-cap stocks are the largest companies typically worth 10 billion or more. When we think of the S & P 500 index or the Dow Jones Industrial Average, we are primarily considering stocks in the large cap category. For most U.S investors, large cap U.S. stocks are the core of your investment portfolio. Small-cap stocks are typically valued at 2 billion or less and mid-cap stocks fill the gap in between. Small and mid-cap stocks might be more volatile due to their smaller size, but they might offer more growth potential as well. Smaller companies tend to earn more of their revenue domestically, so geopolitics and currency valuations might play less of a role in how they perform over given time frames.

Morningstar Equity Style Box™

Large Value	Large Blend	Large Growth
Mid Value	Mid Blend	Mid Growth
Small Value	Small Blend	Small Growth

There are two main categories of international stock: developed markets and emerging markets. As a CPA, a major difference I see between developed and emerging markets relates to financial accounting standards. Developed markets like Europe, Australia, and Japan have financial data that is generally more transparent to U.S. economic users than emerging markets like China. Emerging markets, as their name implies, have high growth characteristics but are also volatile. Both developed and emerging market stocks may fall into the categories of large, mid, or small-cap.

A recent investing concept that has garnered both praise and criticism is sustainable investing. The Certified Financial Analyst Institute defines sustainable investing as a style of investing that balances traditional investing with environmental, social, and governance-related (ESG) insights to improve long-term outcomes (https://www.cfainstitute.org/en/research/esg-investing/sustainable-investing). Some question the wisdom and relevance of trying to apply these concepts to the investment selection process. Others believe that considering ESG criteria is the right thing to do and that companies with strong ESG characteristics are also likely to make better long-term investments. Is there evidence to suggest that incorporating ESG improves or detracts from performance? The data is mixed and subjective, and even proponents of sustainable investing will agree that there is not a universal standard in place to gauge how responsible, ethical, or sustainable a company may be. If you are interested in sustainable investing, let your advisor know specifically what you hope to achieve. There are dozens of characteristics to consider and only a few may be of concern to you (climate change, human rights, religious values, etc.). A fund labeled "ESG" may or may not do what you hope it does.

Is one style of stock better than the others? What makes this question difficult to answer is that each of these styles have noticeably outperformed and underperformed other asset classes over long stretches of time at various points in history. Theoretically, smaller companies and emerging markets could provide the greatest return given their higher risk level. More risk, more reward, right? This often has not been the case, however. You would like to think that taking risk in small and emerging companies would pay off in the long run, but it is impossible to know how these asset classes will perform. In the end, it might turn out that a more conservative portfolio would have performed equally well without all the drama associated with higher risk assets. We don't have a crystal ball, which is why we diversify.

BONDS

Bonds are debt issued by institutions like corporations and governments to raise capital. When you own a bond, imagine yourself as a bank. When you buy and hold a bond, you're entitled to interest payments and when the bond matures, the principal is returned to you. If your bond is from a high-quality issuer who will pay you back in short amount of time, you will receive relatively small interest payments. If your bond is a longer-term bond from a company experiencing financial challenges, you should be compensated with higher interest payments.

Two major factors affecting bonds are credit quality and duration. Credit quality is a measure of a bond issuers financial strength. The highest credit quality issuers carry "A" ratings and above (with the U.S government being the highest with a AAA rating), while lower quality issues may be B rated or be considered below investment grade. Duration is a measure of a bond's price sensitivity to interest rate changes.

If you buy and hold a bond until it matures, you will receive your principal back at the time of maturity. In practice, most investors own bonds through funds that rarely hold until maturity. A bond fund manager will actively buy and sell bonds on a secondary marketplace in search of good deals to improve the total return of their portfolios. If yields on new bonds increase, the value of an existing bond portfolio will decrease. Why would anyone want your old bonds if the new bonds are paying more interest, right? To sell the old bonds, they must be sold at a discount of their face value. This is how bond portfolios can lose money. The reverse also is true when interest rates decrease: your old bonds will sell at a premium and your portfolio will increase in value.

PASSIVE VS ACTIVE

An actively managed fund is a fund that relies on a management team to create a carefully crafted portfolio in hopes of outperforming a given investment index. A passively managed fund has a team that creates a portfolio that is expected to replicate the performance of an index. The active fund is more expensive than a similar passive fund because more research, effort, and professional judgement is needed to select specific investments. To outperform the passive fund, the active fund must outperform by at least as much as the difference in their management fees.

Cost is but one challenge facing active stock managers today. If you follow the stock market at all, you are probably familiar with the S & P 500 index. The companies in this index are the top 500 U.S. companies ranked by market capitalization (i.e., size). Less commonly known is an index called the Wilshire 5,000. The Wilshire 5,000 includes all U.S. stocks with a readily available stock price (excluding penny stocks and thinly traded companies). When the index was launched in 1974, there were approximately 5,000 companies that qualified for the index. By the late 1990's the index grew to over 7,500 companies. A funny thing has happened, however. As of year-end 2021, the index was down to 3,678 companies (American Enterprise Institute. "The Vanishing Stock Market." https://www.aei.org/economics/the-vanishing-stock-market/). How did this happen? Is this something to be concerned with? The answer to these questions is debatable, but one thing is clear: an active stock picker in the U.S. market has about half as many stocks to choose from today as they did a few decades ago.

I have participated in hundreds of conversations with active managers over the years about their performance relative to their respective benchmarks. Some managers have done well, but most have failed to match their benchmark- even before accounting for fees. It is difficult to conclude why, exactly. The most widely known explanation for active manager underperformance is probably the efficient market hypothesis. According to the efficient market hypothesis, current stock prices reflect all available information for a company. Modern accounting standards and technology have enabled high quality information to be disseminated quickly. According to efficient market hypothesis, any move in stock prices is the result of new information. Proponents of the efficient market theory believe that the market is so accurately priced that investors won't be able to consistently find undervalued stocks.

Is there a benefit to including active management in your portfolio? The answer depends partly on how much you believe in the efficient market hypothesis. It might be that the efficient market hypothesis behaves differently depending on the asset class in question. Publicly traded companies in developed markets adhere to strict financial reporting requirements and trade on established, liquid securities marketplaces. High liquidity and data quality bolster the efficient market argument here. Emerging markets companies, on the other hand, may have less certain financial data. Could an active manager find better opportunities there than a passive investment strategy?

Ironically, a mistake some investors make is trying to time the market using passive funds. If you believe a professional active manager can't beat the market, why do you think you can? Thanks to modern investing apps, it is inexpensive to make terrible financial decisions. Your decision to use active or passive management isn't going to make or break your retirement. I have seen retirement plans fail because of extraordinary circumstances and poor planning, not because someone paid half a percent more in fees.

ALTERNATIVES & ANNUITIES

Stocks and bonds are the dominant asset classes of traditional investment portfolios. Where can investors go for diversification beyond stocks and bonds? A third class, "alternatives", is sometimes used to further diversify portfolios. There are a wide variety of alternative assets out there, and they can be confusing to both amateurs and professionals alike. Alternatives can be volatile assets like commodities and cryptocurrency, but they can also be relatively low or medium risk assets like commercial loans, real estate, structured notes, and options-based funds. In addition to diversification, some alternatives like real estate and publicly traded partnerships may offer tax benefits. While alternative asset classes are potentially effective diversifiers, they are also complex and might have liquidity restrictions and high management fees.

Annuities are another tool that can help diversify someone's portfolio. Annuities can be confusing because they come in many shapes and sizes. What they all have in common is that they are contracts issued by insurance companies and offer a blend of protection and growth. They are complex, typically have liquidity restrictions, and may contain riders with fees attached to them.

When some people think of annuities, they image something that looks and smells a lot like a pension. When an annuity is turned into an income stream, this is referred to as "annuitization". Like a pension, the income stream can be for either one person's life, joint life for spouses, or a term certain. A single premium immediate annuity is an immediate income stream purchased with a one-time lump sum. A deferred annuity is an annuity purchased with a lump sum that can be annuitized in the future after a deferral period. During this deferral period, the goal is for the annuity value and income stream to grow.

While guaranteed income streams are one use for annuities, not all annuities will be turned into income streams. They can also be used as tool for growth with safety features. An annuity will usually have a term of 3 or more years, after which the annuity becomes fully liquid to be held, cashed in, rolled over, or exchanged for a new annuity by the purchaser. The insurance company issuing the annuity will typically allow limited access to the funds during the term. Annuities with liquidity restrictions are not an appropriate choice for someone who may need access to the funds. Contracts with longer terms might offer more competitive growth opportunities.

It is important to make a distinction between fixed and variable annuities. A fixed annuity is an annuity that guarantees a fixed interest rate to a purchaser for a specified term. This can be appealing to someone looking for safety of principal and a guaranteed fixed growth rate. These products are generally conservative, do not have management fees, and typically compete with the interest rate products offered by banks. Another type of fixed annuity featuring safety of principal is an indexed annuity. With an indexed annuity, the growth isn't a fixed rate but is instead tied to a market index. These products might offer more growth potential than a fixed annuity, but they do not guarantee a return.

Variable annuities do not offer safety of principal but instead have subaccounts that go up and down in value like mutual funds. Unlike fixed annuities, variable annuities have fees that must be considered. A variable annuity will typically be more expensive than a similar fund. Why would you go with the variable annuity instead of a mutual fund if it is more expensive? A variable annuity might make sense if it has features that provide protection of some kind. Often, a variable annuity will feature a rider that guarantees a minimum level of income. The idea is to give the purchaser of the annuity a chance to participate in the market while guaranteeing a minimum level of lifetime income should market returns disappoint. These riders can be expensive and confusing, but they may offer a purchaser some protection from outliving their assets.

Fixed and Variable annuities are suitable for long-term investing, such as retirement investing. Gains from tax-deferred investments are taxable as ordinary income upon withdrawal. Withdrawals made prior to age 59 ½ are subject to a 10% IRS penalty tax and surrender charges may apply. Variable annuities are subject to market risk and may lose value. Guarantees are based on the claims paying ability of the issuing company.

What is the downside to alternatives and annuities? The answer is usually some combination of liquidity restrictions, product complexity, commissions, fees, and possible loss of principal. Additionally, annuities are not federally insured, relying instead on the financial strength of the insurance company issuing the contract. If you're interested in annuities or alternatives, take your time to review them closely and discuss them with a qualified financial advisor before purchasing.

COLLEGE PLANNING

For many, having grandchildren is one of the great joys of retirement. The arrival of grandchildren often occurs in the years leading up to retirement, and college savings strategies are a popular topic for proud new grandparents. With more people waiting longer to have children, it is common to have children going to college as their parents' retirements are beginning. College savings strategies may even be used by retirees who have a desire to expand their own educational horizons.

Higher education is expensive, unfortunately. The first step of college planning is trying to figure out how much college will cost. Factors like going to school out of state, choosing between public and private schools, and the type of accommodations the student resides in make a large impact. Cheaper does not automatically mean better. It all depends on the needs of student. Be sure to factor in the cost of books, supplies, travel, and other considerations. The American Opportunity Tax Credit and Lifelong Learning Credit may help cover expenses, but there are eligibility requirements you must meet and these credits are subject to phase-outs as your income exceeds certain levels. Employer Educational Assistance Programs and student loan interest deductions are also available to help subject to guidelines. Like a lot of tax-related subjects, higher education is a frequent source of debate and change. Discuss strategies with an advisor to make sure your plans are consistent with the latest laws.

A popular type of college savings plan is the 529 plan. Prior to investing in a 529 Plan, investors should consider whether the investor's or designated beneficiary's home state offers any state tax or other state benefits such as financial aid, scholarship funds, and protection from creditors that are only available for investments in such state's qualified tuition program. Withdrawals used for qualified expenses are federally tax free. Tax treatment at the state level may vary. Please consult with your tax advisor before investing.

There are two types of 529 plans: prepaid tuition plans that are designed to lock in today's prices and college savings plans that allows tax-deferred growth with tax-free distributions if the proceeds are used toward higher education expenses. A lifetime limit of $10,000 can be used from a 529 plan to pay off student loan debt. A donor can contribute up to 5 times the annual gift tax exclusion to a 529 account. This can be a valuable component of one's estate planning strategy, as the contribution will not count against the lifetime gift tax applicable credit.

Some are reluctant to start a 529 plan because they're not certain their child will go to college. What are the consequences if funds are eventually pulled out for something other than school? A distribution from a 529 plan is one part principal, and another part earnings. The earnings portion of a distribution is included in taxable income plus a 10% additional tax penalty. The penalty may be waived in certain circumstances like death, disability, or the beneficiary receiving a scholarship. If the named beneficiary doesn't need the 529 plan, the beneficiary can be changed.

Other tools that might be used to help pay for college include Coverdell Educations Savings Accounts, custodial accounts, savings bonds, government grants, student loans, life insurance loans, and home equity borrowing. Withdrawals from traditional IRA's before age 59.5 will create taxable income, but the 10% penalty will be waived if the funds withdrawn are spent on higher education expenses of the taxpayer, their spouse, or one of their children or grandchildren. Roth IRA's can also be used before age 59.5 for higher education expenses. Roth IRA distributions are not taxable to the extent they are a return of the owner's original contribution. If the distribution exceeds the Roth IRA's original contribution and is deemed a nonqualified distribution, then it will count as taxable income- but the 10% penalty will be waived for higher education expenses. IRA's are intended for retirement spending, be careful not to deplete them.

The Free Application for Federal Student Aid (FAFSA) is used to help determine what options and awards are available to students. Financial aid packages may include grants, scholarships, loans, and other choices depending on a student's family financial situation. Financial aid eligibility is determined by an Expected Family Contribution (EFC) calculation. Income and assets of both the student and parents are taken into consideration. Assets owned by other relatives will not count against the EFC calculation, however distributions for college from relative-owned accounts reduce financial aid eligibility by 50% of the distribution amount. This reduction doesn't occur for two years, however. It makes sense then for grandparents and other relatives to wait to make their distributions in the final two years of college so that the EFC calculation isn't impacted.

LIFE INSURANCE & LONG-TERM CARE INSURANCE

Ideally, liabilities like mortgages are paid off as you approach retirement, your needs simplify, and your dependents become self-sufficient. Is this always the case? More and more retirees are finding uses for life insurance. The good news is that rates may be affordable if you're in good health, don't use tobacco, and aren't involved in any activities a life insurer would deem "risky". Term insurance might be ideal because it is usually the most affordable option. As its name implies, term life carries a fixed cost for a specified period of time (10 years, 15 years, 20 years, etc.). Once the term ends, the policy owner will typically cease making payments. If term life insurance is the solution to the temporary problem of "if" you die, permanent life insurance is the solution to the permanent problem of "when" you die. Permanent life insurance may cost more, but it is designed to leave a death benefit to your heirs whether you live for 6 more months or 6 more decades.

There are several types of permanent life insurance: whole life, variable life, and universal life. What they have in common is that they set aside a portion of your premium payment to grow and eventually build a cash value. In the future, policy owners may choose to access the cash value in the form of a policy surrender or loan. Loans from life policies may have lower rates than current market and provide a source of tax-free liquidity. This can be an appealing source of funding, especially to someone in a higher tax bracket. Outstanding loans will reduce the death benefit payable and cash surrender value and will be taxable income to the extent that there is a gain in the policy.

Where the types of permanent life insurance differ is in how policies are funded and how the cash value grows. Whole life insurance earns interest and premiums remain level. Variable life insurance also has level premiums, but the cash value and death benefit will vary based on the performance of selected investment options. These investments are typically considered securities and policies contain a prospectus. Universal life differs in that the premiums are flexible so that the policy face amount and premium can change based on need and circumstance. Some universal life policies may be linked to a market index like the S & P 500. This will allow the policy to capture some of the growth of a market index while providing a specified level of protection. A variable universal life insurance policy combines the investment choices of a variable life policy with the flexible premium feature of the universal life policy.

With so many options, choosing the right policy can be difficult. Do you need coverage for more than a specific period of time? Are flexible premiums important to you? Are you comfortable with investment risk in your life insurance policy?

Before you retire, you also need to consider long-term care insurance. According to LongTermCare.gov, almost 70% of people turning age 65 today will eventually need some form of long-term care. It is smart to look into long-term care insurance before retirement because the longer you wait, the more expensive it gets. A long-term care insurance policy provides a known benefit for a specified period of time and benefits may be received tax-free if it is a tax-qualified policy. In some states, stand-alone long-term care insurance policies may be part of partnership-qualified programs. These programs help ease the spend-down provisions that are required to be met before an insured is eligible for Medicaid. How important is this? Generally, an individual cannot qualify for Medicaid if they have more than $2,000 in assets. By easing the spend-down provision, the insured retains more of their assets while still qualifying for Medicaid.

Potential buyers of long-term care insurance may be deterred by both the cost of insurance as well as the "use it or lose it" nature of the product. You could easily spend tens of thousands of dollars over many years on a policy that you will never use. An appealing alternative may be permanent life insurance with a long-term care rider. This type of life insurance policy will pay out a benefit if the long-term care component is triggered during the insured's lifetime. This will likely cost more than a long-term care policy, but if long-term care is never needed then a death benefit will go to your heirs.

ANTICIPATING THE FUTURE

I do not have a crystal ball. I can only speculate what stock market returns will be over the next decade or what inflation will look like going forward. I am generally skeptical of those who make bold predictions. From what I've seen, there are no experts who consistently predict the future. We do know, however, that establishing good financial habits has helped millions of people achieve success. Good habits help you control what is within your power to control.

Do your current habits support your long-term goals? Imagine where you want your life story to take you in the future. What actions must you consistently take to get there? If we define our goals well and prepare for a wide variety of possible outcomes, we greatly increase our chances of success. The objective of pre-retirement planning is to prepare us for the next chapter of our story, the day we retire.

| 2 |

THE DAY YOU RETIRE

This is the point in your life story where you finally enter a new field of adventure- retirement! This new field is at once exciting and terrifying. What if the market crashes and you can't make your money back? What if you deplete your assets too soon? What if you can't keep pace with inflation? If at some point your financial situation feels like you are being circled by sharks in the water, remember that shark attacks only kill 6 people a year on average, worldwide. The threat can feel greater than the reality.

Retirement can be scary and there are risks that need to be managed. The first piece of good news is that you are not alone. As people live longer and healthier lives, bigger and better communities form to serve their members. By staying active and learning you are giving yourself the best opportunity to live a long, healthy, and well-funded life. Reading this book is a great start to your retirement journey. The more prepared you are, the more confident you will be in your decision making. Read books, listen to podcasts, and speak with advisors when you feel you may benefit. It is important to hear a variety of opinions, think critically, and carefully form an opinion of your own. No one is an expert on everything, and even those who are experts often disagree with other experts. Even if you outsource some of your decision making to an advisor, you will be the one who owns the results.

HEALTH INSURANCE

Once you're retired, your most important job is to do everything you can to keep yourself healthy. This is a book about financial planning, not fitness. However, health is a major variable that can make or break your financial plans. It saddens me to see clients who did a fantastic job saving and making good financial decisions struggle with quality of life in retirement due to health ailments. Some of this is an unavoidable part of the aging process. Some are luckier than others with health. However, there are always proactive steps you can take to improve your odds of living a long, enjoyable life. Take responsibility and do what's within your power to make positive change for yourself. Exercise. Eat healthy. Challenge your mind.

Are you considering retirement before Medicare eligibility? It is crucial to consider your health care expenses after retiring. If you were receiving a good deal from your employer-sponsored health insurance plan, you may get sticker shock seeing rates in the health insurance marketplace. Tax credits might be available to help offset the cost, but this may be phased out if you have taxable income from pensions, retirement accounts, and other sources. One alternative may be a Health Savings Account (HSA). HSA's are available on certain high deductible health insurance plans. Contributions to the HSA are tax deductible and distributions for qualified health care expenses are nontaxable. Contributions are limited by an amount that increases each year. HSA's can also be funded by a one-time, tax free qualified HSA funding distribution from an IRA. The qualified

HSA funding distribution must abide by certain rules and is subject to the same contribution limits as normal HSA contributions.

Once you reach age 65, you will be eligible for coverage through the federal health insurance program Medicare. Medicare may also be available to certain younger people with disabilities and people with end-stage renal disease. It is best to sign up for Medicare parts A & B in the window that starts 3 months before the month you turn 65 and ends 3 months after your 65th birthday. You could face penalties and coverage gaps if you wait beyond this window. If you reach Medicare age and you or your spouse are still employed and want to stay on your employer's group health plan, be sure to check with your insurance provider to make sure you are eligible to delay Medicare enrollment. Medicare consists of a few different parts.

- Part A- Hospital Insurance. This covers hospital stays, hospice care, and contains limited coverage for home health care and skilled nursing facilities. Part A is free if you or your spouse paid enough Medicare taxes while working, which covers the vast majority of people.
- Part B- Medical Insurance. Covers outpatient care, doctors' visits, supplies, and preventative services. Most people will pay a standard premium amount, with some paying a higher amount if their income exceeds certain thresholds. This additional premium is known as an Income Related Monthly Adjustment Amount (IRMAA) and is determined based on your IRS reported premium from 2 years ago.
- Part C- Medicare Advantage. Private plans offered Medicare-approved health insurance companies that fill gaps in coverage.
- Part D- Prescription Drug Coverage. Part D is optional and requires that you join a Medicare-approved plan.

An important decision you will need to make when you sign up for Medicare is whether to purchase a Medicare Advantage plan, Medigap supplemental insurance, and/or Medicare Part D. Medicare health coverage includes deductibles and coinsurance that you must pay out of pocket. A 20% coinsurance on large medical expenses like heart surgery can leave you with a huge bill. Plans known as Medigap policies are available to help cover these gaps in coverage. Medigap policies are not designed to work with Medicare Advantage plans. You can have one or the other, not both. Your options may vary based on what state you live in. It is best to find a licensed insurance agent who specializes in these products and knows how to match an appropriate plan to your anticipated needs.

NEW ROUTINES

Sometimes recent retirees tell me they don't how they got anything done back when they were working. When you're working a full-time job and dealing with life's day to day challenges, it's easy to get busy and disorganized. After you've retired, you might have more time on your hands. Use that time effectively- get out there, be active, and live your adventure. On a less adventurous note, retirement is also a great opportunity to get your finances organized. It's best to get started early. Presumably, your mind is sharp right now. You are a competent person and savvy decision maker. Don't take that for granted because cognitive decline might impact your abilities in the future. If you get your organized now and maintain good habits, it will help you and your loved ones out immensely in the future.

How much will your budget change in retirement? When financial planners model retirement income needs in our software, we often anticipate that your income needs in retirement will be 70-85% what the were prior to retirement. You don't want to assume expenses will go down once you're retired, however. If you're not working, you've got more time on your hands and more opportunities to spend money. As you might imagine, the actual income figure can be very different from one person to the next. A common scenario is for new retirees to spend more in the early years of their retirement while they're at their healthiest and most active.

What do you anticipate doing with your time when you retire? In my experience, the happiest retirees are the ones who fill their time with purposeful activities. This can take several forms: working part-time at a job they find enjoyable, volunteering, and recreation to name a few. For some retirees, part of your journey will be pushing yourself to try new things.

TRAVEL

Many retirees view travel as one of the new opportunities available to them. It is said that American workers don't take enough vacation days. Perhaps we love work, or maybe we're scared someone else will outwork us while we're away. When you're retired, you have one less excuse not to travel.

One of the best parts of my job is when I can help someone realize that they can afford to make adventures happen. A lot of people with the means to travel struggle to determine how much time and money they're comfortable setting aside for it. They have often accumulated large sums of money in part by being frugal. The idea of spending lots of money on travel may feel strange if you've made a habit of putting it off. I have found that I am able to help people in situations like this. When creating a retirement needs analysis, we can see how your financial situation looks under a variety of scenarios including longer than expected life spans, volatile markets, and increased discretionary spending. Modeling these scenarios allows us to fund a comfortable "splurge zone". We help our client's monitor their financial situations to help ensure that their splurges aren't threatening their long-term goals. It could be that a few bad years in the stock market might force you to downsize your vacation plans. A few good market years may allow you to extend your stay.

There's no one right way to travel. Some retirees prefer the ease of a cruise or all-inclusive resort. Others prefer more of an authentic, local experience. Some want a lavish weekend getaway, other will travel for months on end on a modest budget. Part of the fund is learning about the many possibilities. If you are having trouble getting started planning, here are a few good questions to ask yourself:

- Where are your "must visit" destinations?
- What places would you enjoy visiting, but can live without?
- How long would it take to see everything you want to see?
- How will you get there?
- What type of lodging do you prefer?
- How long do you want to stay?
- Will you travel in a group or solo?
- Do you require any special amenities or accommodations?
- Are there any safety concerns that must be addressed?
- What activities do you want to try?
- Do you prefer relaxation, adventure, or some of each?

A popular way to get deals on travel is to use credit cards with rewards programs and enticing sign-up bonuses. Signing up for a travel rewards credit card allows you to earn points that can be redeemed for things like flights, hotels, and rental cars after you've reach required spending levels. The catch is that there is usually a minimum amount of spending needed to get the bonus and the cards often have an annual fee. You must value the reward benefits enough to justify any annual fee and be comfortable with the terms and conditions of signing a credit card agreement.

Understandably, many people are reluctant to sign up for credit cards because they want to avoid debt and getting roped into a bad deal. In their quest to get organized, many people don't want to put up with tracking a credit card account either. Many fear that opening too many credit card accounts is bad for your credit. It is true that opening multiple accounts in a short period of time can lower your credit score. However, having high credit availability, timely payment history, and a low balance is great for your credit. In my personal experience, having multiple credit cards has helped my credit.

If you think a rewards program could help you meet your travel goals, there are two important rules to follow:

1. Always pay your balance in full and on time so that you are not accruing interest and penalties. If you accrue interest expenses, you are offsetting the benefits you gain from being in the rewards program. Set up automatic payments if possible.
2. Don't open more accounts than you can keep track of it. The more accounts you must track, the more likely you are to miss a payment. Keep a list of accounts.

If you decide to go with a travel rewards credit card, it is best to find a few good cards and rewards programs that you will stick with for the long run and supplement them with the occasional new card and sign-up bonus. Many cards have an annual fee but also come with benefits for being a member like free hotel nights or frequent flyer miles. What benefits could you see yourself using on an annual basis? Sometimes a card with good annual benefits is better than the card with the higher sign-up bonus.

While some people want to see every corner of the world, others are perfectly happy going back to the same vacation spot every year. If there is a place you find yourself revisiting every year, the thought of a vacation home may have crossed your mind.

To make a vacation home affordable, many people purchase vacation homes and rent them out part of the year for extra income. This can be an effective way to offset some of the expenses of ownership. If you are considering a vacation home as an investment play, know that it can sometimes be difficult for vacation rental owners to get considerable personal use of their properties and still make a profit. If your intention is to make a smart financial investment, you may have to avoid personal use of the property to meet your income goals. You must be prepared to pay for service, maintenance, repairs, and renovations. Either you will be doing a lot work yourself to manage the property, or you will be paying a property manager. A property might be a great vacation home or a great investment property- but not always both simultaneously. A vacation home makes the most sense when you can clearly afford to purchase it, maintain it, and you're not under financial pressure to rent it out for income. If you must depend on renting it out to make the finances work, it may not be what you were hoping for. All that being said, many savvy real estate investors have done well for themselves. Know your market.

SOCIAL SECURITY

You can't talk about retiring without talking about social security. Will social security even be around when you retire? There is no question that funding the social security program is a serious challenge. The ratio of workers to retirees has shrunk dramatically since social security's inception. People are living longer too, which means they receive benefits longer. Despite these challenges, Social

Security is an overwhelmingly popular program and I can't imagine it going away.

For social security to remain solvent, something may have to give. One possible outcome is that inflation adjustments to social security benefits will not keep pace with the inflation of the items that most directly affect retirees. For example, your social security might go up 3% one year while your healthcare expenses go up 8%. Another factor that many overlook is how American wage growth has been relatively stagnant compared to the social security wage base. What might this mean to you? If you made $100,000 in 2019 and $100,000 again in 2020, your income is identical in absolute terms. However, for purposes of calculating your future social security benefits, it is not about how much you earn in absolute terms. Your future benefit is calculated based on how much you earn relative to the social security wage base. Social Security benefit amounts are based on a workers lifetime earnings record. The Social Security Administration uses your earnings to calculates a "Primary Insurance Amount", which is a figure based on your earnings compared to the wage base. Every year, the social security wage base increases. If the wage base increases at a greater rate than your earnings do, your future social security benefit may be reduced even if your wages are steady or growing slowly. The exact calculation will depend on your earnings history.

One of your biggest retirement decisions is when you decide to start receiving social security benefits. Full retirement age is the age at which you can get 100% of your Primary Insurance Amount from social security. The age at which you are eligible for full retirement is slightly different depending on what year you were born. If you were born in 1937 or earlier, full retirement age is 65. For those born after 1937, the full retirement age increases gradually depending on what year you were born. For those born in 1960 or later, the full retirement age is 67.

You can take your social security retirement benefits as early as age 62. If you are still earning income, the benefit will be reduced for each month that a worker is younger than their full retirement age. Benefits are reduced by 5/9 of 1% of the primary insurance amount for the first thirty-six months under full retirement age and 5/12 of 1% primary insurance amount or any month(s) beyond the first thirty-six months. A worker can also delay taking social security benefits to receive a larger benefit until the age of 70.

Imagine for a moment that you've retired and started taking social security benefits before full retirement age. Your former employer calls and begs you, "please come back for another year!" If you are thinking about saying "yes" and going to back to work, it is important to understand how this will affect your retirement benefits. If you have earned income and receive retirement benefits from Social Security before reaching full retirement age, your retirement benefits will be temporarily reduced if your earnings exceed certain limits. Social Security has rules meant to deter people from simultaneously working and receiving early retirement benefits. For this purpose, we're specifically looking at "earned" income. This refers to income earned as employee wages or self-employment income. Unearned income, like income from investments and passive income from real estate rentals, won't count against you. This reduction is calculated on monthly basis in relation to an individual's age relative to their full retirement age. If you are under full retirement age, $1 of benefits is lost for every $2 earned once you surpass a threshold. In the year that full retirement age is reached $1 of benefits is lost for every $3 earned above the threshold. While this threshold adjusts for inflation each year, it is relatively low threshold.

When your spouse turns age 62 they are eligible for a retirement benefit based on your earnings record. This benefit is typically 50% of your primary insurance amount at your spouse's full retirement age. If your spouse's earnings record entitles them to a higher benefit, they can take the higher benefit instead. A spouse may be able to get Social Security benefits before age 62 if they're caring for a dependent child who meets certain qualifications. The dependent child must be under age 18, or age 18 or 19 and a full-time student. The child can also be age 18 or over if they were disabled before age 22. Retirement benefits are also available to children meeting these criteria. There is a maximum family limit that applies if the total benefits payable exceeds certain thresholds. A divorced spouse may be able to claim retirement benefits at age 62 if the marriage lasted at least 10 years.

Most Americans take social security early at the age of 62. Is this a wise decision? To answer that question, consider several factors. What is your life expectancy? You must live into your mid-eighties before you reach a breakeven. Consider family health history and that people are generally living longer now than in the past. Are you married? When one spouse dies, the biggest check stays in the family for the survivor. If one of you is the primary breadwinner, this could be an important factor in deciding to holdout. What are the chances one of you will live until your late eighties or beyond? For some, the decision is relatively clear. When the choice isn't clear, consider speaking with an advisor with access to tools that model different social security scenarios.

For an estimate of your Social Security retirement benefits, check out the online calculator and other tools at the Social Security website.

https://www.ssa.gov/benefits/retirement/

ENTREPRENEURSHIP

Some people take on business ownership early in their careers, but for numerous reasons many do it later on in life. Sometimes people have a new boss that they don't enjoy working with. Sadly, I've spoken with many retirees who feel their former places of business has changed for the worse. Many also feel they have been pushed out due their age. It may also be that you are simply ready to try something new. Change is part of life and especially part of business, and it could be that your talents are better served in a new setting where you have more autonomy.

Are you considering a transition to consulting work or self-employment as you ease toward retirement? This is a common scenario, and this type of change requires a shift in thinking if you are a wage-earning employee transitioning to self-employment. This can be an exciting time! It can also be stressful. There are pros and cons to self-employment, and I'm excited to offer a few ideas to help make it work for you should choose to go this route.

Once you decide to go self-employed, you will need to ask yourself how to best organize your business. If you are new to running a business, this can feel confusing. I'll try my best to give you a brief run-down of the business entity types available to choose from.

SOLE PROPRIETORSHIPS & PARTNERSHIPS

Anyone who runs an unincorporated business by themselves is a sole proprietor. Sole proprietorships are relatively simple to manage, and income and expenses can be reported on your personal 1040 tax return Schedule C. If you operate an unincorporated business with one or more partners, you will need to apply for an employer tax identification number and file a partnership tax return in addition to your personal tax return. The relative ease of sole proprietorships makes them popular, but there are good reasons to consider other business entity classifications.

LIMITED LIABILITY COMPANIES (LLC)-

LLCs are a type of business entity that combines characteristics of sole proprietorships, partnerships, and corporations. When it comes time to do your taxes, LLCs are considered sole proprietorships or partnerships unless they elect to be treated as a corporation. Forming an LLC will help protect personal assets from any business legal issues that may arise. LLC rules vary by state, so speak with an advisor who is knowledgeable about how they're treated in your jurisdiction.

CORPORATIONS-

A corporation is a legal entity separate from its owners. Like LLCs, corporations offer limited liability protection for owners. Forming a corporation requires filing articles of incorporation with your state and adherence to a variety of legal formalities.

The most common type of corporation is a C Corporation. One of the best parts of being a C corporation is that there are no restrictions on ownership. This makes it an ideal choice for a person or group who is looking to grow their company by taking on new investors. A disadvantage of C corporations is that they are taxed twice: once at the corporate level and again when shareholders receive dividends.

Most of the retirees I work with aren't trying to grow their company by taking on new investors. For smaller businesses that can tolerate ownership restrictions, an S corporation can make more sense. S Corporations are a business entity that creates a unique status of business owner/employee. Unlike C Corporations, they are limited to at most 100 shareholders who must be U.S. citizens. An S Corporation avoids the double taxation of C Corporations and may lower a sole proprietor's taxable income. A sole proprietor's entire income is subject to self-employment tax. When the sole proprietor changes business entities to an S Corporation, their income will be divided up between employee wages (subject to employment taxes) and dividends. The dividends are not subject to employment taxes, creating a tax savings.

S Corporation shareholder/owners must pay themselves a reasonable salary. The lower the salary, the less employment taxes are paid. The IRS is aware that people will try to reduce their salary to avoid employment taxes. Speak with a tax advisor to help determine a reasonable salary.

You want the S corporation entity to pay business expenses directly. For S corporation owner/employees who might pay business expenses out of pocket, qualified accountable plans may be a useful tool. Qualified accountable plans allow employees and business owner/employees to be reimbursed for out-of-pocket expenses without having to include the reimbursements as taxable income. A qualified accountable plan requires legitimate business expenses and expense reports to substantiate them. Reimbursements should be made within 30 days of the expenditure. If the qualified plan isn't adhered to properly, the reimbursements may be recharacterized as taxable wages by the IRS.

If you like the tax advantages of S corporations but want to minimize some of the legal formalities, consider forming an LLC instead. If you have an LLC, you do not need to be an S Corporation to be taxed like one. An LLC can make an election to be treated as an S-Corporation by the IRS.

Before forming a corporation, consider the additional record-keeping responsibilities. Extra care is needed to separate your business and personal expenditures. You will have to prepare a separate business entity tax return in addition to your personal tax return. You will have to hire a payroll provider and pay yourself a salary. The tax savings must be worth the time, effort, and expenses incurred.

SMALL BUSINESS TAX DEDUCTIONS

There are a number of tax strategies available to help small business owners. Below is a short list of deductions and strategies that I want to highlight for all new business owners. Speak with a tax advisor who understands your business to make sure that these or any other strategies are right for you.

HOME OFFICE DEDUCTION-

Do you have a place in your home that you can dedicate exclusively to regular business use? Is it your primary place of business? If so, you open some exciting tax possibilities. Having office space in your home allows you to deduct a variety of home related expenses, including utilities, home insurance, repairs, maintenance, and depreciation. Home expenses that are typically deductible as itemized deductions, like real estate taxes and mortgage interest, are split between the home office and Schedule A. The deduction is based on the square footage of your office divided by the square footage of your house.

Taxpayers have historically been reluctant to take the home office deduction, fearing that it may somehow be a red flag to the IRS. Home offices are common now. You shouldn't be worried about a red flag, but you should be sure to speak with your tax advisor and make sure you are adhering to the rules entitling you to the deduction. You should be aware that if you take a depreciation deduction related to your home office, you may face a depreciation recapture tax if and when you sell the home in the future. This will occur if the home sale proceeds (minus expenses) exceed your adjusted basis in the home. These figures can be difficult to determine, and it is best to consult a qualified tax advisor. You avoid depreciation recapture on your home office for the years you elect make a safe harbor election. When you take the home office safe harbor election, you simply multiply the square footage of your home office by an IRS-prescribed dollar amount ($5 per square foot as of 2021). Typically, the safe harbor election yields a smaller tax deduction, but avoids recapture and eases recordkeeping responsibilities.

If you have both a formal business location and a home office, you might still be able to take the home office deduction if your home office is your primary administrative office. It's worth stating again that you should review these strategies with a qualified tax advisor who is up to date with the latest tax laws.

MILEAGE DEDUCTION-

One of the best things about the home office deduction is that it empowers you to take full advantage of the mileage deduction. Typically, driving to work or to visit a local client is considered a non-deductible commuting expense. When you have a home office, you can take a mileage deduction for traveling from your home office to your work location. It's important that you make your home office your first stop. If you want a legitimate tax deduction, start your workday with administrative work in your home office before traveling to other business locations. For mileage to be deductible, you must be going from one business location to another. Otherwise, it is a nondeductible commute. Be sure to always document the date of your trip, the location, the miles, and the business purpose. When reporting mileage on your tax return, you will need to track the number of business miles, commuting miles, and total miles.

There are two common ways to deduct mileage: standard mileage rates and the actual expense method. There are nuances involved that you need to discuss with your tax advisor. In practice, most people take the standard mileage deduction, particularly if they are driving a smaller vehicle. With standard mileage, you multiply the number of business miles by an IRS prescribed amount that changes each year. Standard mileage is easier to use and may give a better deduction than tracking actual expenses. When using the actual expense method, there is more record keeping but it is worth it when the actual expenses are high. The actual expense method is typically most useful for businesses with trucks and larger vehicles that spend a lot on fuel, supplies, and maintenance expenses. If you elect standard mileage, you can switch to the actual expense method in a future tax year. Once you elect the actual expense method, you cannot switch to standard mileage in future years.

TRAVEL EXPENSE DEDUCTION-

For travel to be deductible, there must be a clear business purpose. Common examples of business travel are business meetings, potential mergers and acquisitions, and conferences. Hotels, flights, and local transportation are common examples of deductible travel expenses.

Are you open to mixing business activities into a vacation? In practice, many people are already mixing business activities into their vacations but fail to take the deduction due to the mixed nature of their trip. With planning and forethought, you might be able to legally recover some of the cost of your trip by way of a tax deduction. If your trip is primarily intended for quality time with family and friends, don't ruin in it by forcing business into the picture. If travel is a productive way to inject life into your business venture, however, be sure to speak with a tax advisor who is up to date with the latest rules.

When travel is 100% business, understanding deductible travel expenses is relatively straight-forward. It gets tricky when your trip is part business, part vacation. There is even a different set of rules for travel within the U.S. and travel outside the U.S. Generally, rules for travel within the U.S. mainly focus on whether or not your trip was primarily business or primarily personal. If your trip is primarily for business, 100% of the cost of getting to and from your destination may be deductible. Rules for travel outside the U.S. use more specific percentage allocations of business days and personal days. Favorable rules exist for non-U.S. trips that are no more than a week or less than 25% personal time. Be prepared to defend your deduction by maintaining a log of time spent on business activities.

When determining how much of your trip is business and personal, remember to count "standby days" as business days. An often-overlooked aspect of travel tax planning, standby days are weekends, holidays, and other necessary days that fall between business days. If you have business days on a Friday and the following Monday, the Saturday and Sunday between them may each be countable as business days. You now have 4 countable business days instead of 2. Standby days could be the deciding factor in calculating whether your travel is primarily business or personal.

If you are bringing family on the trip with you, their costs are typically nondeductible personal expenses. Can you think of a legitimate business purpose for them to serve? If they have formal job duties and you compensate them, you might be able to justify a tax deduction.

Meals with clients or employees are 50% deductible if there is a business purpose. A 100% deduction is available if the meals are provided on the employer's premises for the employer's convenience or if the meals are available to the public as part of a promotion. Meals may fall under the category of business gifts, which are allowable at a 100% deduction up to $25 to any one individual per tax year. While you can deduct meals at a nice restaurant, lavish or extravagant expenses, sporting event tickets, and club dues are typically not allowed. Additionally, under the Tax Cuts and Jobs Act entertainment deductions were eliminated.

SELF-EMPLOYED HEALTH INSURANCE DEDUCTION-

If you or your spouse are not covered by an employer-sponsor health care plan, you can use the self-employed health insurance deduction to deduct your insurance premiums. Sole proprietors pay their health insurer directly and report the deduction on their 1040. If you are a 2% or greater shareholder of an S-Corporation, you can either be reimbursed by the S-Corporation for health insurance premiums or the S-Corporation can pay them directly for you. The cost is deductible by the S-Corporation, is included as W-2 wages (FICA exempt), and deductible to the shareholder under the self-employed health insurance deduction. Since partnerships do not pay salary to partners, the insurance premiums are reported to partners as guaranteed payments instead of wages. The premium is deductible to the partnership and the individual partner takes the self-employed health insurance deduction.

Home meeting space deduction- Do you have a U.S.-based primary residence or vacation home that could serve your business as a space for company meetings or client events? You can rent your primary home or vacation home for up to 14 days each year and exclude the rental income from your taxable income. Not only can you exclude the income, but the rental expense can be taken as a business tax deduction. Write up a formal lease agreement and document the business purpose of the rental. Research comparable local venues to determine a reasonable fair rent value.

HIRE YOUR KIDS-

Are you as sole proprietor or a 2-person business partner with your spouse? Do you have children are who capable of performing legitimate services for the business? Consider hiring them and pay them a reasonable wage for age-appropriate work. One of the major perks of hiring your children is that you don't have to pay payroll or unemployment taxes for them if they are under 18 years old. You will be able to deduct their wages from your business income. Their wages presumably will be taxed at a 0% effective rate given the standard deduction. This strategy is also a great way to teach them about work ethic and entrepreneurship. If this sounds interesting to you, be sure to research the laws in your jurisdiction. You will need to track their hours, pay them fairly, and write out a contract detailing their age-appropriate job duties. In many places, you can hire your own children if they are at least age 7. You will need to complete IRS form W-4 and include them on a payroll tax return.

RETIREMENT NEEDS ANALYSIS- REASSESSMENT

Hopefully, several years before retirement you did a needs analysis that gave you an idea of what to expect in the years to come. A retirement needs analysis is not a static document. You will need to revisit it periodically, and retirement is a perfect time to do so. In the years before retirement, it is less clear what financial position you will be in when retirement arrives. It is impossible to know exactly what the stock market will do or how inflation will affect you. For better or worse, this will affect your ability to achieve your retirement goals. Now that you've reached the day of retirement, you should have a clearer picture of what your net worth is. You should also have a clearer idea of what your budget it is.

As your journey progresses you will eventually transition from the wealth accumulation phase to the wealth distribution phase. As you do so, you must be more mindful of market risk and consider measures to reduce risk within your portfolio. The goal of diversification is to realize the greatest amount of return per unit of risk. Increasing the number of asset classes in a portfolio may decrease the overall level of risk. Upon retirement, it is common to reduce stock exposure and increase bonds and alternatives.

As you re-evaluate your needs, you might ask yourself, "Should I roll my employer-sponsored plan over to an IRA?" This is a common question new retiree's ask. Which type of account best achieves your goals and maximizes your opportunities? Like most things in financial planning, the answer is highly dependent on the individual. Further complicating the issue is that every employer sponsored plan is unique and is governed by its own plan document. Different plans have different rules regarding important matters like in-service withdrawals and beneficiary distributions. Key considerations when evaluating a rollover:

- Fees
- Investment options
- Account monitoring
- Beneficiary planning options
- Income and distribution options
- Loan and withdrawal options
- Service
- Consolidation of assets

If you are retiring and you have a pension, you will have some important decisions to make. Married with a pension? On one hand, you can choose a single life expectancy option, taking a maximum monthly income for the rest of your life. When you die, the pension benefit goes away. On the other hand, you can take the joint life expectancy option, which is a substantially reduced income so that the pension benefit can remain with your surviving spouse if you pre-decease them.

There are a several obvious problems here. If both spouses live a long life, the lost income from a reduced benefit will add up greatly over time. If both spouses die within a short time of each other, there will be little benefit realized for even having a pension. Furthermore, children and other heirs may not inherit any of the benefits.

There are several alternatives to consider here. Your income options often include something called a "term certain". If you choose to be paid over a single life expectancy, you may also be able to select a term certain guaranteeing that income will continue to your surviving spouse for a specified amount of time. Choosing a term certain represents a middle ground between the single and joint life expectancy options. If you choose a single life expectancy option with a 10-year term certain and die in year 3, your surviving spouse will continue to receive benefits for 7 more years. If you die after the term certain has passed, nothing will pay out.

Is leaving money to heirs important to you? An alternative to consider is choosing the higher-paying single life expectancy income and using a portion of if to buy a permanent life insurance policy. When looking at your pension income choices, subtract the joint life expectancy income amount from the single life expectancy income amount. How much life insurance could you purchase with this savings? The answer depends on your health status and your ability to obtain life insurance at a reasonable rate. If your goal is leaving money to a non-spouse beneficiary, you may be able to get a greater value purchasing survivorship life insurance. Survivorship life policies pay out when the second spouse dies. It is generally more affordable because at least one spouse is likely to live a long time.

How much life insurance do you need? Life insurance has a wide variety of uses and applications. For this specific application, you might purchase an amount of permanent life insurance that will provide your heirs with a similar monthly income benefit as your pension. Part of the challenge here is projecting how much of a lump sum you need from a life insurance death benefit. Remember that one of the great things about life insurance is that the death benefit is nontaxable. Another consideration is how the death benefit proceeds will be used. If it's reinvested, your heirs can use financial modeling software or work with an advisor to calculate a sustainable withdrawal rate that equals your desired benefit. This process is similar to a needs analysis, where you use an assumed rate of growth and inflation.

Note that I said "permanent" life insurance. This contrasts with term life insurance, which is used to insure your life for a specific period of time (10 years, 20 years, etc.). Since you are likely to outlive a term insurance life policy, the cost is less. The cost savings may be enticing to you, so consider what it is that you want your life policy to do for your heirs. Term life is typically used by people who are concerned about replacing lost income to cover large debts like a mortgage or business loan. Permanent life insurance expires when you do, whether that's now or in 50 years. You buy term life insurance to protect yourself from the unexpected and permanent life insurance to prepare for the inevitable.

ESTATE PLANNING

A common mistake new retirees make is assuming that estate planning is something that only "wealthy" people do. Anyone with a spouse, dependents, substantial assets, or charitable objectives will benefit from estate planning. Estate planning is a process of accumulating, managing, and transferring wealth. It may be that your estate planning needs are simple. For many, however, there are complex issues involved. This may include divorce, business interests, special needs, and important relationships that aren't prioritized by existing estate laws. Additionally, the estate planning process can bring up complex emotions. With complexity comes the temptation for many to put this process off. Complex emotions, paperwork, a lack of deadlines, and potential legal fees can all combine to create a perfect storm of procrastination. Can you be one of the proud few who address their estate planning needs before waiting until the last minute?

Smart estate planning should account for the efficient transfer of assets given a variety of costs. These costs may include:

1. Transfer taxes
2. Cost of documents
3. Cost of probate
4. Cost of professional guidance
5. Opportunity costs

A well-crafted estate plan will efficiently transfer assets to your intended beneficiaries in the manner you wish at as low a cost to you as possible. The plan should account for a range of scenarios that include the possibility of you becoming incapacitated. It should also consider timing. It is possible for some estates- even substantial ones- to eliminate probate costs and delays altogether. Potential issues could arise based on how property is titled and how beneficiaries are named in contracts and will.

The greatest benefit of estate planning is peace of mind. With peace of mind comes confidence and strength. At this stage of your journey, there are simple steps you can take to get your plan together. Getting your plan in place early will free you up to better enjoy your retirement to its fullest.

To properly plan, take inventory of your goals, beneficiaries, assets, and liabilities:

1. Family information (beneficiaries, dates of birth, relevant information)

2. List of assets and liabilities
3. Insurance information (health, disability, life)
4. Annuities
5. Wills and Trusts
6. Powers of Attorney or Appointment
7. Tax Returns
8. A list goals and priorities

Due to the complexity of estate planning, you will want to have a professional team in place. Common team members commonly include:

1. An attorney
2. An accountant
3. An Insurance Agent
4. A Financial Planner

Good team members should specialize in estate planning and understand their role. As a CFP® and CPA, for example, I can help explain many of the aspects of estate planning- but I cannot draft legal documents for you. You must hire an attorney to do that. Your team members do not have to be experts in every single aspect of estate planning. Few people are. They should be experts in at least one important domain (law, tax, insurance, investments, etc.) and have enough broad estate planning knowledge to comprehend the recommendations of other team members. A good team will help you stay organized, accountable, proactive, educated, and confident.

You've probably heard before that you need to have a will. A properly drafted will can name an executor, designate guardians for minors, and transfer property to anyone you wish. If you die without drafting a will, it is known legally as dying "intestate". Are you comfortable letting state law decide how your assets are distributed?

If you die intestate, a probate court will direct how your assets are distributed according to state intestacy laws.

To make a will you must generally be at least 18 years old and be of sound mind. Soundness of mind (aka "testamentary capacity") includes the ability to understand the nature of the act of making a will, the will-makers property, and the ability to understand the relationships affected. There must also be the absence of fraud and undue influence. Each state has different rules about what constitutes a valid will. Some states may allow oral (aka "noncupative") wills. Others require a will to be handwritten, signed, and dated. Some may require they be drafted by an attorney. For smaller or sentimental items, consider leaving a letter to your loved ones indicating who you would like to receive which items to avoid cluttering the will.

Although the importance of a will shouldn't be understated, it is also important to know that good estate planning should maximize instruments that pass outside a will to avoid probate. For some assets, you name a designated beneficiary. For everything else, you can name your desired heirs in your will.

When it comes to naming beneficiaries, be familiar with the terms "per stirpes" and "per capita". The terms per stirpes and per capita translate to "by the roots" and "by the head". These designations have important implications when naming beneficiaries. When making a per stirpes designation, the named beneficiaries heirs receive the property at your death should the named beneficiary predecease you. Consider this hypothetical example: imagine you have two children- Ava and Eva- that you name 50/50 beneficiaries of your IRA. Ava and Eva both have two children and spouses. While on a family kayaking vacation, you and Eva are tragically swallowed by a humpback whale. If Eva was listed as a per capita beneficiary, Ava will receive 100% of the IRA. If Eva was listed as a per stirpes beneficiary, Eva's spouse and children will receive Eva's 50% share and Ava will receive the other 50%.

Here's a question for you: if terminally ill and incapacitated, would you want your doctors to "pull the plug"? As you cross the threshold into retirement, you need to give some thought to such unpleasant possibilities. A living will or advance medical directive is used to communicate your wish to end life-sustaining treatments in a narrow range of specified medical situations. Living wills and advance medical directives must conform to state statute and might only be allowed for terminal patients depending on what state you live in.

Importantly, living wills and advance medical directives do not appoint a decision maker for you. To appoint a medical decision maker, you need a durable power of attorney for health care that conforms to your state laws. "Durable" indicates that the power of attorney remains in effect even after you become incapacitated. Some states may not allow a health care power of attorney to end life-sustaining treatments.

A durable power of attorney can also be used for property. Without a power of attorney, the ability to make crucial decisions on your behalf may fall to someone you didn't intend. Remember that giving someone power of attorney means that you are giving them power to act as an agent in your name. You can revoke a durable power of attorney at any time if you are of sound mind. A power of attorney is a position of great trust, so consider your choice wisely. By granting someone this power, you will be responsible for the decisions they make on your behalf.

RETIREMENT REBIRTH

Once you've taken care of your financial and estate plans, you'll have more time to focus on the fun parts of your retirement journey. If you are working at this point in your life, hopefully you are doing so on your own terms. Once you have entered this stage, your goal is to either stay retired or work doing something you love to do. Now should be an exciting moment of rebirth and rejuvenation. Rebirth doesn't have to be expensive, but there is no doubt that money and good financial planning opens doors to transformative and fulfilling experiences. One of the best parts of my job is talking to my clients about the new experiences they're having in retirement. Grandchildren, vacations, new hobbies, etc. Money isn't everything, but it makes a difference. I want you to have as many opportunities for personal growth as possible, and money can empower you to experience these things. If you get these opportunities, cherish them.

Estate Planning Checklist:

- Will
- Name beneficiaries
- Revocable living trust
- Living Will & Medical Power of Attorney
- Financial Power of Attorney
- Insurance Policies
- Social Security Card
- Birth, marriage, and divorce certificates
- Prenuptial agreement
- Titles & property deeds
- List of assets & key contacts
- Logins & passwords
- Funeral Instructions

| 3 |

FINANCIAL CHALLENGES RETIREES FACE

In Greek mythology, there is a character named Sisyphus who angered the gods by cheating death. As punishment, the gods condemned him to the repetitive, meaningless task of pushing a boulder up a mountain. Every time he pushed the boulder to the top of the mountain, it would roll down, and he would then have to start all over. This was to go on and on- for eternity.

After we've experienced a certain amount of heartbreak, turmoil, and plain old wear and tear, we may begin to see ourselves in the character Sisyphus. Facing adversity is part of all our journeys. Instead of seeing Sisyphus as the victim of condemnation, can we reimagine him as a hero? That is what the French philosopher Albert Camus asked of us in his 1942 essay, "The Myth of Sisyphus." Much of Albert Camus's writing revolved around the inherent conflict between a human being's desire to find meaning in life and the fact that life can sometimes feel meaningless. He argued that to give in to this feeling was a form of suicide, and that one must constantly revolt against it. "The struggle itself is enough to fill a man's heart. One must imagine Sisyphus happy," said Camus.

The respected business author Peter Drucker often stated that if problems are the only thing being discussed, opportunities will die of neglect. We certainly have problems to address along our journey, but we should strive to keep our problems in perspective. It is only human for us to feel like Sisyphus sometimes, confronting problems both old and new, day in and day out as if they were boulders to be pushed up a mountain. Some of our problems will not go away, and we must revolt against the feeling of meaninglessness, filling our hearts as Camus asked of us. Problems need not define us in a country where opportunities exist in rare abundance. Put your problems aside for a moment: what opportunities are available to you today? What opportunities are available in the future if you make small changes in your daily habits? The most inspiring parts of stories are the moments when heroes triumph over adversity. The hero themselves is best positioned to triumph when they can see through the fog of their problems and clearly witness the opportunities available to them. With the right mindset, you may be too busy enjoying the pursuit of new opportunities to dwell on old problems.

CHANGE IS CONSTANT

Problems and opportunities alike both arise from change. Change is constant, and every few years new laws are passed that have a significant impact on retiree's financial plans. In 2021 there was the American Rescue Plan, in 2019 we had the SECURE Act, and in 2017 we had the Tax Cuts and Jobs Act, just to name some recent examples. Financial planning is not a set-it and forget-it task. It requires periodic monitoring and re-evaluation. Change is one of the things that makes a financial advisor's job interesting, challenging, and sometimes frustrating. Investment advice can become obsolete in the blink of an eye. Speak with a qualified advisor who is up to date on the latest industry standards and understands your specific financial goals. While this book is intended to give good, lasting advice, be aware that laws can change and revising portions of the text may be necessary in the future.

One of the biggest changes retirees can make is getting divorced, married, or remarried. This can be especially complicated later in life when both spouses have accumulated significant assets. Careful thought must go into how assets will be titled and how beneficiaries are named on financial accounts. Getting married later in life is common and can be a wonderful part of your journey. While we might think of divorce as a sad event, this can also be a perfect example of turning a problem into an opportunity. Presumably, the divorce happened for a good reason. This can be a great opportunity for both parties to start fresh.

If you're getting married or remarried, a prenuptial agreement may sound unromantic. They can provide protection for both you and your heirs, however. A prenuptial agreement will state that each spouse will receive property specified in the agreement instead of receiving their statutory share. This could prevent costly legal fees in the future and ensure that a court isn't dictating how your assets are distributed. The agreement must provide comprehensive disclosure of each spouse's assets and liabilities. Not everyone will be comfortable with a prenuptial agreement, but it serves a specific planning purpose and may be worth your consideration.

Another thing that is sure to change is your health. As you age your lifestyle and financial plans will have to adapt to new realities. Your home may require costly modifications, your medication prices may go up, and your vacation expenses may go down. When you are making financial decisions (home renovations, new vehicles, etc.), do you consider your need to adapt as you get older? Also, keep in mind that as you get older and more health problems crop up, it will be more difficult (and maybe impossible) to obtain life or long-term care insurance.

When it comes to financial news, how do you learn about change? We watch the news to learn about what is going on the world, but what we usually get is the worst thing happening in a few specific places at a given moment. When extreme poverty plummets and rare diseases are eradicated, it isn't deemed newsworthy. The news is way too dramatic! Fear is a powerful motivator and attention grabber. Staying informed on the latest financial news can be smart, but it can also be dangerous. Even when the economy and markets are doing well, there are usually data points worth being concerned about. Even well-intentioned people fall into the habit of hyping bad news to grab your attention. The worst financial choices are frequently made when fear clouds our decision-making. Managing risk in an investment portfolio should be a carefully considered long-term process, not a knee-jerk reaction to the latest headlines.

SURVIVING MARKET DOWNTURNS

Fear shouldn't cloud your judgment, but it is true that a lot can go wrong in a short amount of time. Economic trends that last for decades can reverse abruptly. Market highs are historically accompanied by a feeling of exuberance. In fear of missing out on gains, more investors add risk to their portfolios. This exuberance changes to denial, then fear, then depression when markets fall. Historically, this is where many investors hurt themselves by selling when the market is near a low.

Anxiety and reluctance are natural feelings experienced during the best historical buying opportunities. What is the smart way to handle these emotions? In some cases, a down market might be considered a great buying opportunity. It is important to remember that when you stop earning income, you can't capitalize on market downturns like you used to. Retirement might force you to consider that the risk-on on approach that worked out for you in the past might not work for you in the future. Unless you go back to work, sell property, or inherit new money, you will not have that same opportunity to "buy the dip" anymore.

Once you start withdrawing money from your portfolio, market downturns get even harder to tolerate. The risk that withdrawals are made during a period of poor investment performance is known as sequence of return risks. As you withdraw funds, less money is left in your portfolio to catch future appreciation and the magic of compounding starts to work against you.

On the following page, figure A shows how withdrawals during a market downturn may affect your asset balance. Consider a scenario in which a 65-year-old retiree needs to start withdrawing $30,000 annually from their $500,000 portfolio. Over the next 30 years, we assume growth of 6% in an average year. Assume that inflation will average 3% during his hypothetical time frame and that the retiree's income need will increase each year to account for this.

Scenarios A and B both average a 6% return in a given year over a period of 30 years, yet the same portfolio in scenario B lasted the full 30 years while Scenario A ran out of money in the 19th year. This is attributable to market timing, a factor over which you have no control. While the long-term history of markets is overwhelming positive, there have been extended stretches of time that yielded little growth (see 1929-1954, 1966-1982, and 2001-2009). Your long-term financial plans should consider the possibility that challenging market conditions will arise at an inopportune moment.

Figure A: Sequence of Returns Risk Illustrated

($500,000 starting balance/$30,000 initial annual income need/3% annual inflation)

Age	Scenario A		Scenario B		Annual Income Need
	Investment Return	Year End Balance	Investment Return	Year End Balance	
65	-25%	$345,000	20%	$570,000	$30,000
66	-15%	$262,350	20%	$653,100	$30,900
67	0%	$230,523	20%	$751,893	$31,827
68	5%	$209,267	10%	$794,300	$32,782
69	10%	$196,429	10%	$839,965	$33,765
70	10%	$181,293	10%	$889,184	$34,778
71	10%	$163,601	5%	$897,821	$35,822
72	20%	$159,425	0%	$860,925	$36,896
73	20%	$153,307	-15%	$693,783	$38,003
74	20%	$144,825	-25%	$481,194	$39,143
75	-25%	$68,302	20%	$537,115	$40,317
76	-15%	$16,529	20%	$603,012	$41,527
77	0%	$0	20%	$680,841	$42,773
78	5%	$0	10%	$704,869	$44,056

79	10%	$0	10%	$729,978	$45,378
80	10%	$0	10%	$756,237	$46,739
81	10%	$0	5%	$745,908	$48,141
82	20%	$0	0%	$696,322	$49,585
83	20%	$0	-15%	$540,801	$51,073
84	20%	$0	-25%	$352,996	$52,605
85	-25%	$0	20%	$369,411	$54,183
86	-15%	$0	20%	$387,485	$55,809
87	0%	$0	20%	$407,499	$57,483
88	5%	$0	10%	$389,041	$59,208
89	10%	$0	10%	$366,961	$60,984
90	10%	$0	10%	$340,844	$62,813
91	10%	$0	5%	$293,189	$64,698
92	20%	$0	0%	$226,550	$66,639
93	20%	$0	-15%	$123,930	$68,638
94	20%	$0	-25%	$22,250	$70,697

Despite having the same average rate of return over a 30-year period, scenario A runs out of money at age 77 while Scenario B can still meet annual income needs 30 years later at age 94.

OVERCONFIDENCE

Thanks to technology, it's easier than ever for investors to take a do-it-yourself approach. Many investors who have took a passive approach for years have suddenly become more hands on as they approach retirement, especially in bull markets. It is one thing to read about investing and another thing entirely to experience it. There is danger here. If your investments perform poorly, you may be deterred and take too conservative approach in the future, costing you thousands or more in the long run. Behavioral finance research shows that most people tend to move into popular strategies after the gains have been made and exit positions at the wrong time.

Equally dangerous is if you do well in the beginning and grow overconfident. In 1999, psychologists David Dunning and Justin Kruger identified a cognitive bias now known as the Dunning-Kruger effect, a phenomenon in which confidence can be attributed to a lack of knowledge. To recognize one's deficiencies in a given subject, a minimum amount of subject matter knowledge is needed. As one gains subject matter knowledge, they learn to recognize their deficiencies. Upon learning your deficiencies, you grow more capable but less confident until a certain level of mastery is reached. The people with limited knowledge or competence, unaware of their deficiencies, overestimate their expertise. This creates a strange effect where the more knowledgeable you are, the less confident you are until your reach a certain threshold of expertise. A byproduct of this effect is that you have three general population groups:

- Group 1: People who are somewhat knowledgeable, but are lacking confidence
- Group 2: People who are confident, but lacking knowledge
- Group 3: People who are both knowledgeable and confident

If you fall into group number 2 and you perform well, there is a risk that you may falsely attribute too much of your results to skill instead of good luck. Once you believe you have something figured out, it's hard to accept new information that tells you otherwise. This may inspire inappropriate risk taking. The Dunning-Kruger effect reminds us to be vigilantly humble. Humility is not an expression of weakness; it is a prerequisite to strength.

LONG-TERM CARE FUNDING

The thought of losing your independence can be terrifying, and so can the expense that is associated with it. Fortunately, stand-alone long-term care insurance is but one of several alternatives on the market that try to address the long-term care dilemma.

When discussing long-term care funding, it is important to first understand the roles of Medicare and Medicaid. Medicare Part A will help pay for a skilled nursing facility up to a maximum of 100 days. Once your 100 days are up, you have to pay out of pocket until your pockets are empty. As your nest egg runs out, you will need to look to Medicaid. Medicaid is a welfare program jointly funded by state and federal governments to provide medical care for those with limited income and resources. In order to qualify, an individual must spend-down their assets. There are limited exemptions for residences, cars, burial, and business assets, but Medicaid can take these assets from the estate of the recipient if necessary to recover costs incurred. Medicaid will recover assets from the estate only after the surviving spouse passes, but before any other beneficiaries. Can you "gift" assets to someone to meet the spend-down requirements? Medicaid is one step ahead of you. They use a 5-year look-back rule to delay eligibility for those who try to sidestep their rules by gifting assets within 5 years of applying for Medicaid.

What can retirees do to protect their assets from long-term care risks? One option that we've discussed is long-term care insurance, which provides a specified level of protection and may have tax advantages. Life insurance and annuities with long-term care component are also available that will pay a benefit based on a triggering long-term care event. Unlike long-term care insurance, life insurance and annuities can provide a death benefit for your heirs in case a long-term care need never arises. Certain annuities may be helpful in Medicaid planning too. An annuity specifically designed for Medicaid planning will avoid the 5-year lookback treatment if it is irrevocable, non-transferrable, actuarially sound, and provides equal payments throughout its term. This may be especially helpful in situations where there is a healthy spouse who can receive the income while the other qualifies for Medicaid. What's the catch? The primary beneficiary of a Medicaid annuity is the state Medicaid department. Medicaid annuities may be challenging to set up and restrict access to your assets if you need them in the future. Still, they may be a useful tool for the right person.

ACCESSING EQUITY

Since the point of a retirement plan is to provide benefits in retirement, federal laws prevent you from tapping your retirement plan funds early without penalties. The point of this is to encourage saving for retirement and discourage distributions from your plan when you are young. When it comes to retirement plans, age 59.5 is the age at which you are considered retirement age. What if you want to retire earlier than that? There are a few potential work arounds. At age 55, after separation of service, you can take distributions from a qualified plan. You can do this from a qualified plan but not an IRA, so remember this if you are considering a rollover. Before the age of 59 and a half, you're also able to set up substantially equal periodic payments. This can be done with both qualified plans and IRA's. Distributions that are a part of a series of substantially equal periodic payments will not be subject to the 10% penalty tax if they adhere to IRS guidelines. Typically, you must adhere to a distribution schedule that lasts the later of 5 years or until you reach age 59.5.

Depending on the type of plan you have, there are a variety of penalty exceptions that are available if you need to make early distributions. Qualified plans may allow you to take a loan instead of making a distribution. IRA's may allow distributions for higher education expenses or first-time homebuyers. Both qualified plans and IRA's allow limited distributions for medical expenses and the birth or adoption of a new child. Like most financial matters, this is an area subject to change and it is advisable to speak with a qualified advisor who understands your goals and situation.

If you have a portfolio of stocks or other securities in a taxable option, you can liquidate shares to raise cash. What are the tax ramifications? It helps to know your tax bracket. If you are below the 22% federal tax bracket, the long-term capital gains rate is 0%. Imagine that you've recently retired, you do not have a pension, and you haven't started receiving social security benefits. Your income and tax rate will be low, so now might be a good time to liquidate some shares from your taxable account to cover expenses. You will need to know what your cost basis is to calculate your gain and how many shares you can liquidate before entering a higher tax bracket. If you do enter a higher tax bracket, it's not the end of the world. The higher rate only applies to the portion of gain exceeding the lower bracket's threshold.

If you do not wish to liquidate shares, you may be able to obtain a securities-back line of credit (SBLOC). An SBLOC will allow you to access a line of credit collateralized by the securities in a brokerage account. When opening a line of credit there is no taxable event, allowing shareholders to access equity without the tax consequences of liquidation. The loan terms are usually flexible and might offer a more competitive interest rate than other forms of credit. If opening an SBLOC, be sure to understand the lenders terms and conditions. What happens if the value of your underlying securities drops? Lenders may require you to deposit additional cash or sell shares. If you don't keep current on loan payments, the lender might be able to seize securities to cover your balance.

Some retirees may eventually find themselves in the position of having one particularly valuable asset- their home- and not much else. This is especially true later in life as retirees spend down their retirement assets. There are a few ways retirees may be able to use their home equity to fund other goals.

A cash-out refinance is a refinance in which you replace an existing mortgage with a bigger mortgage and pocket the difference between the two. This is typically done to access equity from price appreciation. The obvious downside to this strategy is that you now have a larger debt to pay off. The wisdom of such a strategy depends on how the terms of the new mortgage compare to your existing mortgage and how those funds are used. A home remodel could add more value to your home, or the funds might be used to pay off other, higher-interest debt. Lenders typically require you to maintain at least 20 percent equity in your home. Also weigh the financial effect of closing costs.

A home equity line of credit (HELOC) can be used to borrow money against your home's equity if and when you need it. Interest rates on a HELOC are variable and usually have a draw period in which you only have to pay interest for a specified number of years (principal payments are optional during this period). After the draw period ends, the repayment period begins. The repayment period may last up to 20 years and outstanding interest and principal balances are paid down during this time. HELOC's often have flexible terms, modest closing costs, and lower interest rates than other types of credit lines. For someone who prefers a fixed interest rate and fixed repayment terms, a home equity loan might be used instead.

A unique option available to retirees is the reverse mortgage. With a reverse mortgage, a lender gives you a nonrecourse loan in exchange for equity in your home. Funds are available either in a lump sum, periodic advances, or a line of credit depending on the type of mortgage you get. Reverse mortgages are unique because as long as you or your spouse lives in the home, no payment on the loan balance is required. The home is still your property, and you are still responsible for paying property taxes, insurance, utilities, maintenance, and upkeep. To be eligible, you or your spouse must be at least age 62, and the home must be an owner-occupied primary residence.

Nothing is too good to be true, and reverse mortgages have expensive fees and rules to follow. Lenders are required to issue a total loan cost analysis to borrowers and the Federal Housing Administration requires consumer education as part of the lending process. When the home is sold, refinanced, or the last borrower leaves, dies, or fails to adhere to the loan terms, the loan balance, interest, and loan costs are become due. Any remaining equity is paid to the borrower or their heirs. A deficiency judgment cannot be taken against the borrower, their heirs, or their estate.

Reverse mortgages may not be appropriate unless you have an immediate need for liquidity. As equity in your home is reduced, your liabilities increase- which decreases your net worth. One must weigh their desire for liquidity against their desire to stay debt-free. This can place you in the tricky position of deciding which financial goals to prioritize. What is most important to you? Will a reverse mortgage help you maintain independence? Are your short-term needs being adequately addressed? Consider that you may have less equity to leave behind to others. Also consider how the loan balance will affect your equity should you decide to sell the property in the future.

FRAUD & LIABILITY PROTECTION

While topics like market risk and health concerns may make up most of our worries, the biggest financial risk we face might actually be legal risks. This is especially true once we have accumulated substantial assets. Auto accidents or slip and fall injuries on your property have the potential to create massive legal damages. Liability coverage is typically included on auto and home insurance policies but be sure the coverage limits are high enough to protect your assets. Certain business and recreational activities may be excluded by your personal liability coverage and require an insurance policy of their own. A personal umbrella insurance policy may be purchased to provide coverage when the limits of the underlying insurance policies are exceeded. Insurance policies may also offer coverage for identity theft and cybersecurity.

Sadly, retirees are frequently targets of scams, identity theft, and fraud attempts. Some may seek to exploit vulnerable people on dating websites and social networks. Others may pose as representatives of the IRS, Social Security Administration, or other institutions to try to extract sensitive information. Consumer awareness and improving technological tools help deter scammers, but they adapt their tactics, and we must remain vigilant to protect ourselves.

Undue influence is an important concept to be aware of, especially as physical and cognitive decline emerge later in life. Undue influence is present when someone tries to influence another person to do something they otherwise wouldn't do. This may take the form of duress, physical threats, and emotional threats. Surrounding yourself with a group of people you trust and confide in is a good way to help protect yourself. Perpetrators may act to isolate and control a victim. No one person should have the ability to manipulate you or control access to other perspectives and resources. If you or anyone you know is being abused physically, emotionally, or financially, reach out to your local adult protective services or law enforcement.

LOSING LOVED ONES

Many prefer not to think about death and taxes, yet they seem to be the only thing you can always count on. If you live long enough, you will eventually have to endure the hardship of losing loved ones. Do people make their best financial decisions when they are managing great personal loss? Death hits us hard, especially when it's timing is unanticipated. You can spend decades exercising clear-minded financial discipline and lose your gains in a matter of months, days, or even seconds in a moment of crisis.

Grief may require a long process before you get back to something resembling normal. If you feel that you are a rational decision maker at this present moment, respect the possibility that your rationality might prove tenuous. Starting with her 1969 book, "On Death and Dying," psychiatrist and author Elisabeth Kübler-Ross identified 5 stages of death, grief, and other profound losses. These stages are denial, anger, bargaining, depression, and finally acceptance. Before we arrive at acceptance, the intensity of the preceding stages may cloud our normal judgment. If we are mindful of where we are in the grieving process, we may be able to resist the unwise impulses that lead us astray from our desired journey.

Moments of crisis sometimes come with a side order of legal responsibilities. There may be a time in the future where you become a fiduciary either by court appointment or through an instrument like a trust document. What does this mean to you? Your exact roles and responsibilities vary by the situation, but in general becoming a fiduciary means you will carry ethical and legal responsibilities. Violating your responsibilities could leave you personally liable for damages.

When a loved one passes, they may name an executor as their personal representative in their will. If they die without naming a personal representative, the court will appoint an administrator. Both executors and administrators are examples of fiduciaries, and the titles are sometimes used interchangeably. Trustees named by a trust document are another type of fiduciary. They are responsible for administering a trust and its assets. Executors and administrators must act in the best interests of the estate's beneficiaries, and trustees must do the same for a trust's beneficiaries. Their responsibilities may include safeguarding assets, filing tax returns, communicating with the decedent's creditors and beneficiaries, paying off debts and expenses, and distributing assets.

Being a fiduciary is work. Fiduciaries may be financially compensated either by provisions established in the corresponding legal documents or as decided by a local court. Sometimes fiduciaries decline compensation and choose to receive assets as an inheritance instead. Fiduciary income is taxable and inheriting assets might be tax-free depending on what it is you are inheriting. In addition to the administrative workload, communicating with family and other beneficiaries can prove challenging. Managing the estate of a loved one who has passed is frequently emotional and stressful.

Executor Checklist:

- Notify relevant financial institutions and government agencies
- File the Will with the local probate court
- Gather date of death value statements from the financial institutions
- Satisfy any required minimum distributions
- Get an estate tax ID
- Open an estate account with check writing privileges to pay expenses such as funeral costs, estate settlement costs, pending bills, loan payments, etc. Keep a log of all transactions.
- Make payments to creditors
- Publish the estate in the local newspapers, giving creditors opportunities to notify the estate.
- Hire a realtor if necessary to sell real estate
- Dispose of tangible personal property to intended heirs. Consider an estate sale of any remaining items. Deposit sales proceeds into the estate checking account.
- Notify all beneficiaries of the estate.
- If necessary, prepare an inheritance tax return
- Prepare the decedents final income tax return
- Determine if probate is necessary.
- Distribute the final balance to beneficiaries once all creditors & debts are paid in full. Consider having the beneficiaries sign a release indicating that by accepting their inheritance checks, they will not contest the estate.

OPPORTUNITIES LIE AHEAD

It is easy to be bogged down by problems. They are inevitable and they are everywhere. We've spent chapter 3 discussing many of the challenges you will face in retirement. Good financial habits lay a foundation for you to face these challenges from a position of strength. While problems are everywhere, so too are opportunities. With the right perspective, you increase your odds of achieving success. In chapter 4, we will discuss how to manage success effectively.

| 4 |

MANAGING SUCCESS IN
RETIREMENT

If success was easy, would it make a good story? In the most popular stories, success is only found after a period of exploration and struggle. A hero without a journey isn't particularly interesting.

A period of exploration and struggle preceding success is common in real life as well as in stories. These experiences sharpen our abilities and prepare us to manage success when it arrives. What happens when financial success arrives quickly? We have all heard stories about lottery winners, professional athletes, and others who have lost sizeable fortunes. From the outside looking in, people might ask themselves, "How could these people lose so much money so fast?!" Success is usually the result of good habits cultivated over a long period of time. If the money arrives before your good habits are established, you risk be separated from your money sooner rather than later.

Ideally, we spend our younger years establishing good financial habits. When we are getting started, we work toward a future where we have enough money to fund a sustainable lifestyle. We experience those years believing that once we hit certain financial targets, we can finally relax. I've learned from my conversations with clients and colleagues that as you achieve old goals, you find new things to worry about and new goals to pursue.

Many people are better at making money than keeping it. During peak earning years, you may not notice bad habits emerging because you have more than enough income to prevent any shortfalls in the near term. Without new money, will you have the ability to address new financial needs? When you are working, your proficiency in earning income can mask some of the issues you might have in managing your assets. Without new earned income in retirement, your margin for error decreases radically.

In this chapter we will discuss concepts you should be aware of and steps you can take to manage success.

ACCREDITED INVESTORS

According to the United States Securities and Exchange Commission, some investors are sophisticated enough to invest in certain complex securities that aren't available to everyone. These investors are known as accredited investors. How sophisticated must you be to be considered "accredited"? As long as you have enough income or net worth, you are considered an accredited investor. If your net worth is over $1,000,000, either alone or together with a spouse (or spousal equivalent, excluding your primary residence) you meet the definition. If your earned income exceeds $200,000 alone or $300,000 with a spouse or spousal equivalent in this year and each of the prior two years, you also meet the definition. Accredited investors can also be businesses, trusts, charities, and other institutions.

What does it mean to you to be an accredited investor? There are certain alternative investments you can choose to participate in that aren't available to everyone. This can be good or bad. Accredited investors have a variety of goals just like regular investors. What is the time horizon and risk profile of the asset you're considering? How liquid is it? How sound is the company issuing the investment? What is the minimum investment? Know what you're investing in.

ASSET PROTECTION

As your asset balances rise, so does your need for asset protection. If your brokerage account increased by $1,000,000 in the latest bull market, do you have enough liability protection? With the cost of medical care being what it is, $1,000,000 can go fast if you're held responsible (or even partly responsible) for hurting someone in an accident. As we discussed earlier, a way to increase and broaden your coverage is to purchase an umbrella insurance policy. This will add coverage on top of your underlying home, auto, and other insurance policies. For example, your home insurance may provide up to $500,000 personal liability. Adding a $2 million umbrella policy on top of that would give you a total of $2,500,000 coverage.

If you have a business, you need to take extra steps to protect yourself. Personal umbrella insurance policies often exclude coverage for business activities. There are two general types of coverage that all business owners should be aware of: general liability and professional liability. General liability covers physical risk like bodily injuries and property damage. Professional liability insurance will cover you for any errors and omissions you might make. A common example is malpractice coverage for doctors and lawyers. Anyone can make an honest mistake, and this is where professional liability comes into play. The cost to insure these risks depends largely on the industry you are in, how much experience you have, and whether or not you've had any claims.

If you have employees, you need workers compensation insurance. This will cover medical expenses and lost wages for employees. Most states require workers compensation insurance for all employers.

If you are part of a family business, how might you protect the businesses assets from the creditors of your family members? A family LLC is an entity structure that helps protect family business assets from the claims of creditors against individual shareholders and aids in distributing income to future generations. One family member will act as managing director. The family LLC has an operating agreement that dictates the ownership rights, decision-making authority, and terms of asset transfer. Because the business owns the assets, it is harder for creditors of individual family members to go after these assets. Shares transferred to heirs may also be discounted for estate tax purposes. A common estate planning strategy is to gift shares in small increments each year to gradually reduce the size of the taxable estate. Do their complexity, you will need to see an attorney to properly set up a family LLC

Another type of business entity that many are vaguely familiar with is a shell company. A shell company is a legitimate legal entity that does not actually operate a business. They are mainly used as a means of facilitating financial transactions. Unfortunately, shell companies are notorious for their use in concealing illicit or unethical activity. They are also known for their occasional use as a legal but potentially unethical means of tax avoidance by large corporations.

What are some potential legitimate legal uses of shell corporations? Here are a few:

-acquiring a publicly traded company
-hiding assets from hostile entities
-access to foreign investments

-privacy

-tax savings

Why would a billionaire buy a yacht in the name of a shell corporation? If they wish to sell that yacht in the future, selling a corporation that owns the yacht might have smaller taxes and registration fees than if they sold it outright as an individual owner. Shell company assets may potentially be custodied in the U.S. yet registered as the property of the foreign shell company. The privacy aspect may be especially appealing to high-profile individuals who wish to avoid scrutiny of their personal possessions. In some countries and jurisdictions, governments and criminals may target wealthy individuals.

Those wishing to start a shell company should seek specialized professional advice and consider the cost and ongoing administrative expenses involved. Shell companies are heavily scrutinized. Compliance and the legal environment must be taken seriously.

ROTH CONVERSIONS

It is possible to convert a traditional IRA to a Roth IRA. When does a Roth conversion make sense? If you are in a position where you may be taxed at a lower rate now than in the future, a Roth conversion might make sense. What will your tax rates be in the future? We don't know the exact answer because tax rates can change. However, there are cases when the current cost is likely worth the future benefit. Consider a high-income earner from the 32% federal tax bracket who has recently retired. Perhaps they have no pension, but they can live off savings and after-tax investments for a few years before starting social security. They may find themselves in a 12% bracket temporarily until their social security benefits and required IRA distributions start, at which time they will be bumped up to the 22% bracket. In effect, any amount of income they take in the interim will be taxed at a 10% discount to the extent it falls within the 12% tax bracket. In the long run, this might save them thousands of dollars in taxes. Due to the constraints of tax brackets, Roth conversions are often done incrementally. The idea is to use as much of the lower tax bracket up as you can and stop just short of the next higher bracket. Large conversions can create large tax bills. Remember to add state taxes in too!

When converting an IRA that is funded with 100% deductible contributions, the entirety of the converted amount is taxable income. When converting an IRA that was funded with nondeductible contributions, a portion of the conversion is a nontaxable return of basis. The deductible and nondeductible contributions must be aggregated when determining the portion of your conversion that is taxable, even if they are in separate accounts. The end result is that the amount of a Roth conversion that is free of tax is proportional to the amount of basis in the IRAs.

CONCENTRATED PORTFOLIOS

If your portfolio is heavily concentrated in one particular company or sector, the straight-forward solution is to sell shares and reinvest into a diversified portfolio. The downside is that you will likely incur significant taxes on the sale. The are a few other alternatives, each of which has its own strengths and weaknesses. For publicly traded securities, buying a put option could help reduce risk. A put option is an option that gives you the right to sell your shares at a specific price by a specified expiration date. These are most suitable if you are looking to minimize downside risk for a limited time period. Ideally, your stock performs well, and your put option expires worthless. Although you're down the cost of the put option, this is a good outcome. If your stock value falls however, your put option protects you by giving you the right to sell at the strike price of the put.

Another strategy, if you are charitably inclined, is to donate your security to a Charitable Remainder Trust. If you donate appreciated capital gain property to a CRT, you do not have to pay taxes on the capital gain portion of the donation. In addition, you get a tax deduction. How much of a deduction do you get, you ask? Good question. A donation to a CRT is considered a "split-interest" donation. There are two parts to a split interest donation. One part is an income stream that goes to a beneficiary, which can be yourself or someone else. The income will be paid out over a predetermined time period and will be taxable as ordinary income. The other part of the split interest is the "remainder" portion that goes to the charity after the income time period has passed. This portion is tax deductible and is based on a formula. The greater the income you pay to yourself, the smaller the tax deduction will be. CRTs are complex and take thorough planning, but they are also great tools for the right situation.

Another way to make an impact while reaping tax benefits is by investing capital gain proceeds into a Qualified Opportunity Zone fund. Opportunity Zones are economically distressed areas where new investments may receive tax benefits if certain conditions are met. The goal is to improve these areas by creating incentives for investing in them. Opportunity Zone funds allow investors to defer their capital gains and potentially eliminate capital gains on future appreciation if they hold the investment for 10 years. These funds may be risky and are typically only available to accredited investors.

For non-publicly traded securities, other advanced strategies may include installment sales, private annuities, and self-cancelling installment notes.

ESTATE TAX

The Tax Cuts and Jobs Act of 2017 establish a maximum federal tax rate of 40% for gift tax, estate tax, and generation skipping transfer tax. Fortunately, a generous exemption amount exists, and most people won't have to worry about paying estate taxes. As of 2022, an individual needs over 12 million dollars and a married couple needs over 24 million dollars in their taxable estate before having to pay estate taxes. Estate tax laws can change, however. They are complex and are also frequent subjects of debate. This requires a watchful eye to monitor and anticipate any changes that might occur in the future. Some states have estate or inheritance taxes in addition to the federal estate tax. For those affected by the estate tax, the affect is profound. What tools are available to help mitigate or eliminate the estate tax?

It is important to be familiar with the term portability. Portability refers to the amount of unused exemption remaining after a spouse's death. After the first spouses dies, the surviving spouse may use this remaining portion of the decedent's exemption at their own death in addition to their own exemption.

To illustrate, here is an example:

Assume the exemption amount is 12 million per spouse. The first spouse dies and uses $10 million of their exemption. Because of portability, the remaining $2 million may be added to the surviving spouses exemption amount when they die.

There are a few conditions that need to be met for portability too apply. The decedent spouse must have died after December 31, 2010, and the executor must have filed a timely estate tax return making an election to allow portability. What if the surviving spouse has more than one deceased spouse? Only the unused exemption amount of the last deceased spouse is available. If you had multiple marriages, you can't add up all the exemption amounts to increase your allowable exemption (nice try, though!).

The gross estate includes the value of all property the decedent has interest in at death. This may include property the decedent transferred if they retained certain right or powers over the property. Income in respect of a decedent (IRD) is a category that can be considered both an asset of the taxable estate and taxable income. IRD is income that the decedent had earned and was entitled to and received after death. IRD may include rental income, interest income, annuity payments, and debt forgiveness. One type of IRD- retirement plan or IRA distributions made after death- is taxable as income to the beneficiary at the time of distribution. Between the estate tax and ordinary income tax paid by the beneficiary, over 80% of the value of an IRA may be lost to taxes. IRD assets do not receive a step-up in basis.

Determining the value of assets plays a major role in calculating how much estate tax you have to pay. To properly value some kinds of property, qualified appraisers may be needed to give an independent valuation. There are several techniques you can use to reduce property valuations and the size of your taxable estate. Assets in a taxable estate are typically value at fair market value on the date of your death. An alternative valuation date (AVD) may be used in certain cases to help reduce the value of your estate. To use the AVD, a timely estate tax return must be filed, and all assets are valued as of the AVD except assets that were disposed of after date of death (but before AVD) and "wasting assets" (assets whose values decline automatically with time- patents, annuities, notes, etc.). To use the AVD, the gross estate and its tax liability must be less than what the date of death valuation would have been.

When filing an estate tax return, remember the following deductions:

-Unlimited marital deduction
-Funeral expenses
-Administrative expenses (legal, accounting, appraisals, etc.)
-Unpaid liabilities
-Charitable contributions
-State death taxes

GIFTING STRATEGIES

The federal gift tax exists to prevent people from avoiding the estate tax by giving away their money before they die. Gift taxes can be a confusing topic at first. When first learning about the gift tax, you learn that there is annual exclusion amount ($16,000 for 2022). Many believe that if you gift someone more than the annual exclusion amount, you will have to pay gift taxes. This is only true if you've used up your lifetime gift tax applicable credit. The gift tax applicable credit is $12.06 million (2022), which means you can gift up to $12.06 million (2022) to someone before paying any gift taxes. If you're financially successful, gifting strategies may be a smart way to reduce your taxable estate.

The IRS defines a gift as a completed transfer of an interest in property in exchange for less than full and adequate consideration. Donors making gifts greater than the annual exclusion amount will have to file a federal gift tax return. Gifts taxes are paid by the donor and are not taxable income to the recipient. Gifts from businesses to employees, however, may need to be counted as income to the recipient. Gift taxes only apply to completed lifetime gifts. When making gifts to reduce your taxable estate, you must take care to ensure that your gift is considered a *completed* lifetime gift. If it is not considered a completed lifetime gift, the property may end up in your taxable estate.

Here are some basic rules to follow to make sure your gift is completed successfully:

1. The donor must be competent to make the gift
2. The donor must have the intent to donate
3. There must be actual or constructive delivery of the gift property to the donee or their representative
4. There must be valid acceptance of the gift by the donee

By making a completed gift, you have completely given up control over the property. If your gift is contingent or incomplete, it will remain in your taxable estate. How might an incomplete transfer occur? When the donor retains a right to reclaim the gifted property or maintains control over the property, it is an incomplete gift. An incomplete gift can become completed if the donor releases their control and/or power of revocation. A "gift" made at time of death is considered a testamentary transfer, not a gift. Special rules apply if the gift is made to joint tenancy bank accounts or joint tendency savings bonds. For joint tenancy bank accounts, a gift is not considered completed until gifted funds are withdrawn by the donee. Similarly, a joint tenancy savings bond is not a completed gift until it is redeemed by the donee.

The most common gifting strategy is to gift property annually up to the exclusion amount to your desired donees. Remember, gifts up to your annual exclusion amount do not count against your lifetime gift tax applicable tax credit. Any gift to a donee above the annual exclusion amount is countable against your lifetime gift tax applicable credit. Making gifts under the annual exclusion threshold you can reduce your taxable estate without subjecting yourself to gift taxes. For married couples, the annual exclusion can be doubled to $30,000 per donee if you elect gift splitting with a spouse if your spouse consents to gift splitting. A gift tax return must be filed if gift splitting is elected. Gift splitting is not required for gifting community property or jointly owned property. If choosing between gifting business and nonbusiness assets, consider giving the nonbusiness assets first in case the business asset might qualify for advantageous estate tax treatment

Is it possible to make a gift above the annual exclusion amount without having to worry about gift taxes? Certain gifts are deductible for gift tax purposes. This includes transfers between spouses (gift tax marital deduction) and transfers to qualified charities. If your spouse is not a U.S. Citizen a maximum of $159,000 (for 2021) per year is gift tax-free. Medical payments or tuition payments made directly to a medical or educational institution are considered qualified transfers not subject to gift tax. These payments do not count towards the annual exclusion amount, and they are not limited to family members. A special rule applies for gifts to a 529 college savings plan. A donor can contribute up to 5 times the annual gift tax exclusion to a 529 account. The contribution will not count against the lifetime gift tax applicable credit, but the donor must file a federal gift tax return.

What if you inherit property that you intend to gift to someone else? Instead of receiving the property and gifting it later (subject to gift tax laws), you may be better off making a qualified disclaimer. A qualified disclaimer is a written, irrevocable refusal to accept the property designated to you. Upon refusing the property, the property is passed on without your direction. Since you do not have direction, consider who will end up with the disclaimed property. Often this is a child that would have been your intended beneficiary anyways. The qualified disclaimer is a way to transfer the asset to them without incurring gift tax.

What if, instead of making a gift to a donee, you give them a below-market loan? This is possible, but there are special rules in place to prevent people from abusing this strategy. A gift loan of

$10,000 or less is not subject to gift tax unless the lone proceeds are used by the donee to purchase income producing property. Once you cross that threshold, more rules come into play. Gift loans of $100,000 or less are not subject to gift tax if the donee's net investment income is less than or equal to $1,000. The loan must have a valid purpose other than tax avoidance to receive preferrable gift tax treatment. If interest income exceeds $1,000 on a loan of $100,000 or less, imputed interest will be charged. The loan will be considered a gift from the lender to the extent the federal applicable rate exceeds the actual loan interest charged. If the loan interest is less than or equal to $1,000, there is no imputed interest, and a gift has not been made. For loans greater than $100,000, the imputed rate is used (federal applicable rate less interest charged). Imputed interest on loan from a corporation to a shareholder is characterized as a dividend instead of a gift. Imputed interest on a loan between an employer and employee is counted as compensation, not a gift.

What happens if you give gifts to your grandchildren? You must exercise caution so that you are not subjected to the generation-skipping transfer tax (GSTT). The GSTT is designed to prevent making excess gifts to related individuals two or more generations below the transferor. It will not apply to gifts to a grandchild if their parent is deceased. The GSTT is a tax in addition to gift and estate taxes using a flat rate equal to the highest gift and tax rate in the year of transfer.

PERSONAL PROPERTY & REAL PROPERTY

At this point in your journey, you have likely accumulated valuable possessions. In financial planning, it is helpful to distinguish two types of tangible property: personal property and real property. A distinction should be made because they each have their own set of rules to consider. Real property includes land and personal property that is affixed to it. All other tangible property is considered personal property. Personal property can also be intangible, meaning it is not a physical object. This may include royalties, copyrights, or patents. Intangible assets may also include items that are physically represented with a document or certificate, such as stocks, securities, or confidential business data.

There are long-term financial strategies that are unique to real estate. One of the tax advantages for real estate investors is depreciation. Depreciation allows a tax deduction for the cost basis of your building assets over a period of 27.5 years for residential real estate and 39 years for commercial real estate. Your cost basis is typically the purchase price plus any improvements, with a non-depreciable allocation to land. Depreciation expenses help offset income. Depreciation benefits can be further enjoyed by hiring a qualified firm to do what is known as a cost segregation study. A cost segregation study allows real estate investors to take more depreciation faster by allocating basis to items with shorter depreciation lives. It is important to speak with a qualified tax advisor to see how passive loss rules may impact your ability to take losses on rental real estate. If you are considered a passive real estate investor, your depreciation deduction can only help offset passive income sources.

If you are familiar with investment real estate, you may also be familiar with a 1031 Exchange. A 1031 exchange is a transaction in which you sell a piece of investment real estate and reinvest in like-kind real estate within a specified time frame while utilizing a qualified intermediary. Why go through this trouble? Tax deferral. By making the like-kind investment in new property, you get to defer capital gains and depreciation recapture. This can work great if there is a specific property you wish to acquire. What if you don't feel like managing a new property? Instead of buying a specific property, you can invest in a Delaware Statutory Trust. This trust invests in commercial real estate and qualifies for the tax benefits of the 1031 exchange. This may only be available to accredited investors, and investors must consider the cost, complexity, and risks involved. 1031 exchanges are complex transactions, be sure to discuss these with a qualified tax advisor before committing to one.

JOINT OWNERSHIP & COMMUNITY PROPERTY

When acquiring property, people often don't put much thought into how their property is titled. This can be a huge mistake. Most property is owned fee simple and will pass through probate. As we've discussed, one of the goals of estate planning is to minimize probate expenses. Property titling is an issue where you will really need to communicate directly with your estate planning team. There are a number of potential solutions, each with their own tradeoffs. When implementing these solutions, you must ensure that they conform to the legal standards required in your jurisdiction.

When owning property, particularly if you are married, joint ownership is common. Joint ownership comes in two flavors to be familiar with:

1. Joint tenants with right of survivorship (JTWROS)
2. Tenancy in common

With JTWROS, two or more owners hold an equal fractional interest. When one owner dies, the property passes directly to the surviving owner(s) without probate by operation of law. For nonspousal JTWROS property, a unique gift tax situation could arise if unmarried individuals contributed unequal amounts to the purchase price of the property. In this case, the tenant contributing the greater percentage of the purchase price is considered to have made a gift to the other tenant. This gift is calculated by subtracting the actual amount of the contribution from the equal contribution amount.

In some states, there is a form of JTWROS called tenancy by the entirety that is available to spouses. With tenancy by the entirety, a spouse cannot sever their ownership interest in the joint property without the other spouse's consent. This form of ownership allows greater creditor protection.

For tenancy in common property, ownership percentages may differ and there is no automatic right of survivorship. The tenant can sell, gift, or donate their share. Upon death, the tenants share typically passes through probate. Examples of property held in common may include investments and business interests.

Further complicating the issue of joint ownership in certain states are community property laws for married individuals. In these states, married individuals own an equal and undivided interest in property accumulated during marriage. If you are in a community property state, it is important that your team understands how your specific states laws affect your property. Property acquired before marriage typically won't be considered community property if held separately. Additionally, separately held property acquired during marriage and acquired by way of gift, inheritance, or court award might not be considered community property by your state. What happens to your property when you move to a community property state? Typically, property acquired before your move is still considered separate property. What if you move out of the community property state? Typically, community property will remain community property. Half of all community property is included in the probate and gross estate when the first spouse to dies. To avoid probate at the first spouse's death, some community property states allow a community property with right of survivorship.

LIFE ESTATES

Is leaving your home to heirs important to you? It is for many retirees. Many consider gifting their homes to their heirs during their lifetime, but it may be unwise for numerous reasons. Some people might ask themselves: Is there a way to gift my home during my lifetime while guaranteeing that I can still live there for the rest of my life? You might be able to accomplish this with a life estate. A properly drafted life estate may be useful in Medicaid planning while preserving the valuable step-up in basis for your heirs. Life estate property gives the holder the exclusive right to the use and enjoyment of the property for the remainder of their life or the life of a designated person. Whoever receives the right to use and enjoy the property is known as the life tenant and they are responsible for the upkeep of the property. This means paying any taxes due on the property, making repairs, and providing maintenance if necessary. When a life estate is first set up, the original grantor of the life estate chooses who will receive the property upon the life tenant's death. The grantor may be able to grant the holder of the life estate powers to choose their own remainderman after the holder's death. It may also be possible to maintain a life estate for a specified term instead of your lifetime if that is a more suitable solution for you.

While a life estate may help protect your home for your heirs, there may be tradeoffs to consider. To be eligible for the desired benefits of the life estate, you might be required to relinquish the right to perform certain transactions without your beneficiaries agreeing to them. This could be a problem if you wish to sell or refinance the home and the beneficiaries won't agree to it. Consult a quailed estate attorney who knows the rules in your jurisdiction.

TRUSTS

Trusts can be a confusing topic because there are many kinds of trusts out there. Who needs a trust? Trusts are commonly created to avoid probate expenses, reduce taxes, and manage assets. They may serve specific functions, like protecting benefits for a family member with special needs or owning life insurance to create liquidity for an estate. To properly draft a trust, it is highly advisable to seek out a qualified attorney.

Let's start by understanding what a trust is. A trust is a legal arrangement involving three parties: a grantor, trustee, and beneficiary. The grantor is the person who creates the trust and transfers property (known as principal or corpus in legal-speak) into it. The trustee oversees management and custody of the trust property. They have a fiduciary responsibility to abide by the trust document and distribute corpus and income as indicated. The beneficiary can be one or more people who hold a beneficial interest in the trust. If a beneficiary has an income interest, this means they receive income from the trust assets. If a beneficiary has a remainder interest, this means they receive the trust property when the trust terminates. It is possible for the grantor to serve 2 of the roles or even all three in the case of a grantor trust. A trust's lifespan is dictated by the trust document. Most states allow trust's a long but finite lifespan, with some possibly allowing the trust to last in perpetuity (infinitely).

A trust may be either a living trust (aka "inter vivos") or a testamentary trust. A living trust, as you might guess, is created while a grantor is still alive. Testamentary trusts become effective and irrevocable at the time of death. Property transferred to a living trust before the grantor's death avoids probate. A testamentary trust may not be an appropriate solution if you are trying to avoid probate. With a testamentary trust, assets are typically transferred to the trust through the will and are therefore subject to probate.

Trusts may be either revocable or irrevocable. Revocable trusts can be changed or terminated by the grantor. If a trust is both revocable and living, we call it a revocable living trust. The revocable living trust is revocable during the grantors lifetime and becomes irrevocable at the time of their death. When the grantor transfers property to an irrevocable trust, they give up all control over the property. If property is transferred to an irrevocable living trust during the grantors life the gift tax applies. The gift tax does not apply to property in a testamentary trust, because the gift is not considered made until time of death. This is considered a testamentary transfer.

A grantor trust is a type of trust that gives the grantor certain powers. This may include an interest in the trust income or principal, control over the property, or a power to revoke the trust. If your trust is a grantor trust, you are treated as if you own the assets and the trust is not considered a separate entity for tax purposes.

Non-grantor trusts are considered distinct taxable entities. Compared to individual income taxes, trust income taxes are highly progressive. What this means in tax-speak is that you hit higher tax brackets much sooner on trust income than on personal income. If assets generate income that will be taxed at a higher bracket within a trust, do you really want those assets in the trust? Part of trust planning includes planning for how trust income will be taxed and distributed to beneficiaries.

A trust gets a distribution deduction for distributing income to its beneficiaries. This deduction is the lesser of a) the amount actually distributed, or b) the distributable net income. Distributable net income is a figure used by the IRS to calculate the maximum allowable distribution deduction. Distributions of trust income to the trust beneficiaries are taxable to the trust beneficiaries. Distributable trust income includes normal income and expenses items but does not include items related to the trust corpus (capital gains, depreciation, etc.). A trust is considered "simple" for tax purpose if it does not distribute corpus, has no charitable beneficiaries, and is required to distribute income each year. Any trust that doesn't meet those characteristics is considered a complex trust.

EMBRACING SUCCESS

People love rooting for the underdog. After an underdog achieves victory, they are no longer an underdog. Will you continue to root for them? Humans seem to have a love affair with watching powerful people fall from grace. When our story begins, we may see ourselves as the underdog. Long after we've achieved success, we still remember the underdog within us even when the outside world sees a champion. Eventually, once your journey is clearly a success, you must accept that you will not always be seen by others as the same underdog at the end of your story as you were at the beginning.

Not everyone will applaud your success. To see yourself succeed while people you care about struggle can be hard. Fear of success and self-sabotage are real things that deter some people from fulfilling their potential. Additionally, many people who accomplish great things deal with imposter syndrome, the feeling that they are inadequate even in the face of obvious success. When you rise to new heights, you will make new peers. Your new peers may not recognize the work it took to get you to these new heights. Your old peers may experience feelings of resentment. Adapting to a higher socio-economic standing may come with tension, but it is clearly worth the price of admission. Your presence can inspire others to follow your lead. Be a reminder to your new peers that the space they occupy is special and not to be taken for granted. Show your old peers what is possible.

| 5 |

LEAVING A LEGACY

Death is one of the hardest things to discuss. Is it possible to live life free from the fear of death? I don't know if it's 100% possible, but when we can be at peace with our mortality, it helps bring a clarity of purpose. Freedom from the fear of death grants the ultimate freedom: the freedom to live in the moment. Awareness of death doesn't have to be morbid doom and gloom. If you take the appropriate time now to get your affairs organized, you will be able to experience greater comfort and satisfaction moving forward. In this chapter we will learn about financial strategies that can help you leave a lasting positive impact.

NAMING A FIDUCIARY

Losing people we love is one of the most challenging parts of life. Consider what mental state your beneficiaries will be in when you die. Do people make their best decisions when grieving? Even the financially savvy among us can make bad financial decisions under pressure. The better you prepare during your lifetime, the more likely your loved ones are to weather the storm of your passing.

One of the first things to consider is who you want to manage your estate. This person will act as a fiduciary, meaning they are required to act in the best interest of an estate or trust's beneficiaries and avoid conflicts of interest. If you've ever been a fiduciary, you know it's hard work and a serious responsibility. When naming a fiduciary to represent you after you're gone, ask yourself a few important questions about them. Are they efficient, effective, and organized? Are they able to communicate effectively with family members, business partners, and other relevant parties? Will they have any conflicts of interest in fulfilling their duties?

Fees an executor receives are taxable gross income. Common examples of fiduciaries include executor, administrator, trustee, and guardian. Executors are named in a decedent's will. They must receive letters testamentary from a court authorizing them to act as an executor of the decedent's estate. If there is no will naming an executor, the court will appoint an administrator and give them letters of administration authorizing them as a personal representative of the estate. The terms executor, administrator, and personal representative may be used seemingly interchangeably depending on what state you reside in. Whichever title a fiduciary goes by, they will have an obligation to safeguard the decedent's property and pay the decedent's outstanding taxes, debts, and expenses. Finally, they will oversee distributing assets to the rightful beneficiaries. As you might imagine, being the fiduciary can be stressful, particularly if other parties are putting pressure on them. Fiduciaries who breach their duties may be held personally liable for damages. You can help your eventual fiduciary immensely by making your plans clear and enforceable during your lifetime.

PROBATE

Do you enjoy complex, time consuming, and expensive processes? If so, you might like probate. Probate is a public process that transfers title of your property at death to your beneficiaries. During this process, the validity of your will is proven in court and all parties of interest- including creditors- are given notice of the proceedings. Probate provides an orderly process where creditors are paid and beneficiaries receive clean title to the assets. How long does probate last? It varies, but it usually takes at least 6 months and is commonly a year or longer. Probate costs vary depending on what state you live in. The fee is usually based on a percentage of the assets in the probate estate. What is more annoying than probate? Two probates! If you own real property in multiple states, there may be multiple probate estates to account for. If you own community property without survivorship rights, this property too will pass through probate.

Planning for probate is a great way to make your loved ones lives easier. What steps can you take to minimize or eliminate the pain of probate? Most financial instruments- life insurance, retirement plans, annuities, etc.- will let you name beneficiaries or set up payable/transfer on death instructions. By naming beneficiaries, these assets can be transferred directly without passing through probate. Any property titled joint with rights of survivorship or tenants by entirety will pass automatically to a surviving spouse. Lastly, assets transferred to a living trust before the grantor's death will avoid probate too.

STEP-UP IN BASIS VS. GIFTING ASSETS

One of the most powerful estate planning tools available is the step-up basis. A step-up in basis occurs when the tax basis of your assets increases to its fair market value on the date of your death. Imagine that you've owned shares of stock for a number of years and their value has increased since the day you bought it. If you sell those shares during your lifetime, you owe capital gains tax on the appreciation. The amount of capital gains that you report as taxable income is determined by subtracting your tax basis from the sales proceeds. If you die and your heirs sell those same shares, their tax bill will be much smaller and possibly eliminated because their tax basis increased when you died. When one tenant in a joint owner-ship interest dies, the survivor inherits their share with a step-up in basis. In community property states, there is a step-up in basis for both spouses' shares of community property.

Assets you gift during your lifetime will not receive a step-up in basis when you die. Gifting assets may make sense for your particu-larly situation but remember that you heirs lose the step-up in basis if you do so.

To determine the basis of gifted property, your beneficiaries will need to know your adjusted tax basis. In the simplest situations, the adjusted basis is the amount you paid for the property. The calcu-lation can get more complex quickly. If you are gifting real estate or business property, did you take any depreciation deductions? This will reduce the adjusted basis. If you receive gifted stock, are dividends reinvested? This will increase your tax basis. Calculating basis can be complicated and may require the aid of a qualified accountant.

Further complicating the issue is that there is one method for "gain" gift property and another method for "loss" property. By gain property, I mean property that has appreciated in value. When gifting gain property, the donor's basis and holding period carry over to the donee. A gain is realized if the donee sells the property at a higher price than the carryover basis. When gifting loss prop-erty, a double basis rule applies. When using the double basis rule, basis is unknown until the donee disposes of the gifted property. If the donee sells the property at a higher price than the donor's adjusted basis, the donee uses the donor's holding period and gain is determined subtracting the donor's carryover basis from the sales price. If the donee sells the property for less than its fair market value at the time of gift, a different treatment is used. In this case, the donee calculates their loss using the fair market value at the time of gift. The donee's holding period begins on the date of gift for sale of loss property, not the carryover holding period.

If the donee sells the gifted property at a price that falls between the donor's adjusted tax basis and the fair market value on the date of the gift, no gain or loss is recognized. If the donor paid gift tax when gifting the property to the donee, a portion of the gift tax is added to the property's adjusted basis for gain property. Gift tax will not be allocated to the basis for loss property.

Sometimes gifting strategies are used to reduce taxable estates. Gifting also might be attempted to help qualify for Medicaid eligibility in anticipation of expensive long-term care needs. You might remember, however, that Medicaid has special rules to prevent people from gaming their system, using a 5-year look-back rule to delay eligibility to anyone who gifted assets within the 5-year period. Effective gifting needs to happen 5 years ahead of a Medicaid need.

INHERITED IRAs

When discussing inheritance planning with your heirs, make sure they understand that inherited IRAs belong in their own category. They can't be mixed in with other IRAs. Ideally, your heirs will take their required distributions over as many years as possible to augment the power of tax deferral. A popular strategy for inherited IRAs is called the "Stretch" IRA. This strategy refers to when an IRA beneficiary takes the bare minimum distribution from an inherited IRA over their life expectancy. The compounding effect is a powerful tool for creating large sums of tax-deferred wealth accumulation. Some good things don't last forever, however. The SECURE act took away the ability to stretch IRA assets over many beneficiaries' life expectancies. All beneficiaries who can't meet the definition of an "eligible designated beneficiary" must take withdraw their inherited IRA balance within 10 years.

Your heirs should be made aware that indirect rollovers cannot be used with inherited IRA. An indirect rollover is when you receive funds directly from a retirement account and then deposit them into an IRA within a 60 day window. If you try that with an inherited IRA, the entire lump sum will be taxable income. When transferring money from a decedent's IRA to an heir's inherited IRA, the funds must be transferred directly from trustee to trustee. Inherited IRAs have their own rules and cannot be mingle with traditional IRAs.

An eligible designated beneficiary can use their own life expectancy when calculating required minimum distributions from an inherited an IRA. The following people meet the definition of eligible designated beneficiary:

- Surviving spouse (may also use the original owner's life expectancy)
- A disabled or chronically ill individual
- An individual who is not more than 10 years younger than the IRA owner
- A child of the IRA owner who has not reached the age of majority (upon reaching the age of majority, they will have within 10 years to withdraw the inherited IRA balance)

Employer-sponsored retirement plans might require your heirs to take a distribution over a period of 5 years or less. For some, this may factor into the decision of whether to rollover to an IRA.

Be sure to understand what the tax consequences will be for your beneficiaries and clarify your options with your retirement plan administrator if it's of concern to you.

While required minimum distributions are not required from Roth IRAs, they are required for an inherited Roth IRA. Fortunately for your heirs, the inherited Roth IRA still retains its tax-free treatment. If your primary goal is to leave IRA assets to someone else, consider their tax bracket. It could be the case that you can convert a traditional IRA to a Roth IRA at a lower tax rate now than your heir will have to pay if they take distributions from an inherited traditional IRA in the future. While inherited Roth distributions are not subject to income tax, the balance of a Roth IRA is still an includable part of your taxable estate. Is there even a benefit to converting to a Roth IRA if it is going to end up in your taxable estate? A Roth conversion may still be smart considering that you're effectively prepaying your heir's income taxes while also reducing your taxable estate.

TRUSTS AS BENEFICIARIES

Are you afraid that one of your heirs may spend their inherited IRA too quickly and/or irresponsibly? It's a valid concern for many. You've accumulated these funds over decades of hard work and disciplined investing. Are you confident that your heirs are ready to manage it as responsibly as you'd like them to? How might you exercise control of these assets after you're gone? If your investment company allows it, one possibility might be a Trusteed IRA. A Trusteed IRA is an IRA that will automatically put your IRA in a trust at the time of your death using a pre-drafted trust template. Because a Trusteed IRA is created from a template, it cannot do everything a lawyer-drafted trust can, but it might be a simple solution that fits your needs. It may also suffice as an easy temporary solution until you've had time to research more nuanced options with a qualified estate attorney.

If the trusteed IRA doesn't adequately address your concerns, a qualified estate attorney may draft a trust that can be named as beneficiary of the IRA. This may be appropriate for family businesses, children from previous marriages, and other potentially complicated scenarios. When naming a trust as beneficiary, your attorney should draft it so that your heirs can maximize any potential "stretch" benefits if possible.

In addition to providing control from beyond the grave, trusts may help minimize estate taxes and avoid probate. When it comes to trusts, it helps to know your ABCs:

An A trust, also known as a marital trust, provides a surviving spouse with income for life from the trust property and a remainder interest in the property is distributed after their death to the beneficiaries.

The B Trust, also known as a bypass trust, family trust, or credit shelter trust, is used to take advantage of the estate tax applicable exclusion amount. At the first spouse's death, they leave assets equaling the applicable exclusion amount in the B trust and give the rest to the surviving spouse. Assets in the B trust are included in the first decedent spouses' gross estate and bypass the surviving spouse's gross estate. The assets placed in the B trust are now "frozen" for estate tax purposes, meaning that further price appreciation will not be included in the taxable estate of either spouse.

The C Trust, also known as a qualified terminal interest trust (QTIP), is similar to the A trust but the grantor maintains control after death. This can be helpful to a grantor who wants to control who receives the remainder interest in the property after the surviving spouse dies.

Trusts can surprisingly simple or excruciatingly complicated. When speaking with a qualified estate planning attorney, have a clear idea of what you would like the trust to accomplish. Clearly articulating your wishes will help them find the best available solution for you.

ESTATE LIQUIDITY

Presumably, one must be wealthy to have to worry about estate taxes. However, being wealthy does not automatically mean there will be sufficient cash available at your time of death. Death is expensive: estate taxes, administrative expenses, unpaid liabilities, funeral expenses, and more. What if most of your wealth is comprised of illiquid assets? If an estate is forced to sell assets to pay these estate expenses, there is a chance these assets may sell for less than anticipated.

Life Insurance is a commonly used tool to provide liquidity at time of death. The proceeds from a life insurance policy are income tax free, however they may be included in the taxable estate if the estate was a beneficiary, or if the decedent owned the policy within three years of death. To avoid inclusion in the taxable estate, an irrevocable life insurance trust might be used. This type of trust can be used to loan death benefits to the estate to pay expenses. Death benefits paid to the irrevocable life insurance trust are not included in the taxable estate if the trust was used to originally purchase the life insurance policy or the life insurance policy was transferred to the trust more than three years prior to the date of death.

For owners of farms and closely held businesses, there is an election available to defer payment of the estate tax for 5 years. Interest is paid during the deferral period and after 5 years the estate tax can be paid in 10 annual installments.

DEATH BENEFIT RIDERS

As we age, obtaining life insurance gets more difficult. What options are left when we want protection for our loved ones, but we can no longer qualify for affordable life insurance? For the right person, a possibility might be an annuity with a death benefit rider. An annuity can't use a relatively small amount of money to fund a large death benefit like a life insurance policy can. However, an annuity can include features to protect an investment account's value from market fluctuations. This is sometimes done with death benefit riders that are attached to the annuity contract. Annuities vary greatly from one product to another, and so do death benefit riders. Commonly seen variations of the death benefit rider might include:

- A guarantee that your principal will be repaid upon your death regardless of market performance.
- A guarantee that your investment will grow at a fixed interest rate for a specified number of years.
- A guarantee that your earnings will be locked-in at specified intervals, establishing a new "floor" for your beneficiaries to inherit.

Death benefit riders usually have a fee attached to them. How much is the fee? If it's a fixed percentage, you can multiply that percentage by the contract value to determine its cost. What is the value of the guarantee? This varies by annuity contract. The value may be a fixed dollar amount, or it could be indeterminable. What makes a death benefit rider a good choice? Here are some important factors to consider:

- How much insurance do you already have? Do you want or need extra protection?

- Health history. If you are healthy enough to qualify for competitive life insurance rates, that may be the smarter option.
- Risk Tolerance. Imagine that A) you want to invest in volatile asset classes, and B) your primary goal for a particular bucket of assets is to leave it to a beneficiary. An annuity may allow you the upside opportunity of exposure to a volatile asset class while giving your beneficiaries downside protection with the death benefit rider.

BUSINESS SUCCESSION PLANNING

A question for business owners: what is your business worth without you? Some business owners face a conundrum in that they built their businesses around their own unique persona. Business owners who don't prepare may find themselves in a position where there is no obvious buyer for their business when they are ready to exit. It takes foresight to create a marketable business entity whose perceived value can be successfully transferred to a successor. If you own a business and haven't taken this step, this should be a high priority for you.

Creating a marketable business entity is a huge accomplishment. Once this mission is accomplished, how does a business owner know what it's worth? Many business owners don't know what their business is worth because credible, independent valuations are expensive and take time. Is it worth the hassle? Like so many things, it depends. Businesses in some industries, like insurance agencies and accounting firms, are known to sell within a range of industry standard multiples of gross revenue. For example, an accounting firm earning $1 million gross revenue may sell for $1-$1.5 million dollars. If your business is unique, it may be a challenge finding a buyer, but your business may also present a rare opportunity for the right buyer. Supply and demand uncertainty in an inefficient market creates a wide range of potential outcomes. If someone really wants to buy you out, they may be willing to pay a premium. If forces beyond your control force you to sell when no buyers are ready, you may not walk away with what you feel the business is worth. Don't wait until the last minute to market your business.

Once you have a potential successor identified, consider their competency and motivations. Many people that are good at working in a business as a technician are not as skilled at working on a business as an executive. If your successor fails but you've already cashed out, will it matter to you? In my experience, business owners care greatly about what they've built and the clients they serve. Success is in everyone's best interest.

Selling a business can create a large tax bill in the year of sale. What can business owners do to reduce it? There are a few options that might help.

We talked before about qualified opportunity zone funds (QOZ funds). Reinvesting capital gains from the sale of a business into a QOZ fund will defer capital gains tax and eliminate further capital gains if the QOZ fund is held at least 10 years. There are unique risks and nuances involved, so discuss with a qualified tax advisor.

One way to manage the pain of a large tax bill is to spread it out over a period of time. Installment sales are an agreement to sell the business in installments over a specified term. When done properly, the tax bill is spread out over the installment period, which may help the seller stay in a more favorable tax bracket. Payments received by the seller will be comprised of capital gains, ordinary income, and return of capital. What happens if the buyer struggles and can't make their installment payments to you? Installment agreements often provide for the original owner to take over the business should the seller stop making payments. Obviously, this is not desirable for either party. Even if you retake possession of your business, what state will the business be in if your successor isn't up to the task of managing it properly? Before entering an installment agreement, you should trust the buyer and have a contingency plan. Installment sales may be an appealing option for family businesses when the successor is well-known to you. Remember that since this is a sale, there is no step-up in basis upon the death of the seller.

An alternative to selling a business that may also work well with younger family members is a leaseback agreement. This can be an effective way to transfer income producing property from one generation's estate to the next. This first step of a leaseback is to gift or sell business assets to a younger family member. The business then leases the asset back from them at a commercially reasonable rate. The income they receive from leasing the asset back to you might be taxed at their presumably lower tax bracket and help them pay for the asset.

Family businesses looking to reduce estate tax liabilities might consider a family limited partnership. A family limited partnership is a type of partnership created to transfer assets to younger family members at a reduced valuation and cost. This strategy makes the most sense for operating business with substantial capital assets who would like to reduce their taxable estate. What makes this strategy particularly powerful is valuation discounts on limited partner interests. Typically, children will be named limited partners and are gifted a limited partner interest. Since a limited partner cannot easily sell their interest or manage the business, there is a lack of marketability discount and minority discount applied to their share of the business. The senior owner of the business transfers the business to the family limited partnership and retains control as the general partner. The limited partnership interests are typically gifted over time within the limits of the annual gift tax exclusion amount. Forming a family limited partnership may require the assistance of attorneys to properly set up the entity and appraisers to determine property business valuations.

Are you considering selling your business at less than its fair market value? This is considered a bargain sale, and it consists of one part sale and another part gift. There is a taxable gain for the seller to the extent the sales price exceeds the basis. The difference between the amount the seller receives and the fair market value is considered a gift. The gift amount is eligible for the annual gift tax exclusion and any amount above the exclusion will be considered a taxable gift.

Ideally you will sell your business at a time of your choosing, but what if you die unexpectedly? Buy-sell agreements are often used to guarantee that there is a buyer of the business at the time of death. They are commonly funded with life insurance and can establish the value of a business. The death benefit provides liquidity so that business's continuity is maintained in the aftermath of an owner's death. A cross-purchase agreement is a type of buy-sell agreement where partners purchase life insurance on the lives of each other to ensure they have the funds to buy out the deceased partners share. Life insurance premium payments are not tax deductible, but the life insurance proceeds are not taxable income. A step-up in basis is available at the business owner's death, minimizing or eliminating capital gains for their beneficiaries upon sale. Buy-sell agreements can also be made that are triggered by disability.

PHILANTHROPY & CHARITABLE TAX SAVINGS STRATEGIES

Americans are well known for their giving nature. According to Giving USA, Americans made $484.85 billion in charitable donations in 2021 alone (https://www.nptrust.org/philanthropic-resources/charitable-giving-statistics/).

In addition to charitable giving, many of us are also involved in volunteering and fundraising for charitable causes. When you're building your nest egg in the early stages of your retirement journey, it can be difficult to prioritize charitable giving. For those of us who haven't started giving, it's not too late. What kind of impact would you like to make in your community?

The tax benefits of donating property depend greatly on what kind of property you are giving away and who you are giving that property to. Rules can and do change, so be sure you speak with a qualified tax advisor. Charitable donation deductions are normally limited to 50% of your adjusted gross income (AGI), unless you only give cash, in which case the limit increases to 60% of AGI. If donating appreciated assets- like stocks that have increased in value- to a qualified charity, the limit is 30% of your AGI. Contributions to private foundations are limited to 30 percent of AGI for cash and 20 percent of AGI for long-term publicly traded appreciated securities. What if you donate more than you can deduct in a given year? You are allowed to carry forward your unused deduction 5 years. If you can't use the full value of your deduction in 5 years, you will lose the remainder.

There are few general rules you should be aware of regarding charitable contributions. You can't deduct the value of your time given volunteering for charity, but you can deduct mileage incurred in performing charitable activities. If you donate $250 or more to a single charity, be sure to request a receipt. Cash donations require a receipt or supporting bank records regardless of the amount contributed. Independent appraisals are needed for gifts of property in excess of $5,000 (excluding publicly traded securities). Be aware that you may need to subtract the value of any benefits you received in exchange for your charitable donation (meals, sporting events, etc.) when calculating your deduction.

Starting the year you turn age 70.5, there is a unique way to donate assets from an IRA called a qualified charitable distribution. A qualified charitable distribution is popular because any distributions made directly to a public charity go towards satisfying your annual required minimum distributions. The assets must go directly from your IRA custodian to the charity and are not reported as taxable income on your tax return. You might wonder, how is this better than receiving the distribution directly and then making a charitable contribution? To deduct charitable contributions, you must take itemized deductions, which many people don't do. Also, by leaving the income off your tax return, it may help you reduce your tax bill in other ways like lowering your income threshold for medical expense deductions. Please note, this strategy is specific to IRA's and does not apply to other retirement account types like 401(k)s, 403(b)s, etc.

Do you have any assets like stock or real estate that have appreciated greatly in value? Not only can you deduct the fair market value of the property you give away, but you also get to exclude any taxable gain that would have been realized had you sold the property. That is two tax benefits in one transaction! Please note that this wouldn't work for assets held in retirement accounts.

If you are interested in converting some of your assets into an income stream, there are a few ways to do this while also qualifying for a tax deduction. An idea we discussed earlier was the charitable remainder trust. A charitable remainder trust is a type of irrevocable trust in which the remainder interest is a qualified charity. To execute this strategy, you donate an asset to a charitable remainder trust, receive an income stream from the trust for a period of time and receive a tax deduction in the year of donation based on an IRS formula. The income tax deduction amount is based on the difference between the value of the donated property and the present value of the annuity payments. The income paid from the trust each year is taxed as ordinary income to the donor/grantor.

Charitable remainder trusts come in two basic varieties: the charitable remainder annuity trust and the charitable remainder unitrust. Both types of charitable remainder trust can last for the life of the grantor or for a term up to 20 years. The present value of the charitable remainder interest must be at least 10% of the fair market value of the property transferred to it. The simple way to think about this is that the greater the charitable remainder interest is, the greater the tax deduction is. When setting up a charitable remainder trust, you must weigh the benefit of a larger income stream against the benefit of a larger tax deduction and charitable gift. At least 5% and no more than 50% of the trust fair market value must be paid out each year. A charitable remainder annuity trust pays the grantor either a fixed percentage of the fair market value the donated property or a fixed dollar amount each year. This amount must be paid even if the trust much reach into principal. Charitable remainder annuity trusts allow no additional contributions after inception. The charitable remainder unitrust is more flexible. With a charitable remainder unitrust the grantor receives a fixed percentage of the trust assets each year. The annual income amount may be limited to income earned by the trust so that principal isn't invaded. They may provide for catch up provisions when income does not meet percentage requirements and additional contributions may be allowed.

Two concepts similar to charitable remainder trusts are charitable gift annuities and pooled income funds. Both provide the donor an income stream from a charity in return for an irrevocable transfer of assets. Like the charitable remainder trust, the donor is eligible for an income tax deduction based on the difference between the value of the donated property and the present value of the annuity payments.

Instead of giving directly to a charity, some people prefer starting either a private foundation or donor-advised fund. This allows for more control on the part of the donor. Instead of giving a large sum directly to the charity, funds can be invested and distributed with guidance from the donor as to which charities will receive funds and when. A tax deduction is received in the year a donor gives to the private foundation or donor-advised fund, even if the private foundation or donor-advised fund hasn't given away assets to a charity yet.

Private foundations are tax-exempt charitable organizations typically funded by a family, corporation, or small number of donors. There are two general types of private foundations: operating and nonoperating. Operating private foundations use funds directly in their own charitable work, and nonoperating foundations distribute funds to others for charitable purposes. Private foundations allow the donors control over investments and distribution of assets. Family members may be employees of the foundation or serve on the board. Private foundations are subject to strict, public reporting requirements and may be expensive to manage. A few other disadvantages are that non-publicly traded contributions, such as privately held stock or real estate, may be deductible only at cost basis rather than at fair market value and there is an investment income excise tax of 1.39%.

Is there a less expensive alternative to private foundations that offers many of the same advantages. With a donor-advised fund, a donor gives a gift to a charity or financial institution who then establishes a fund in the donor's name. Once the fund is set up, the donor makes grant recommendations to the fund's administrators. The donor receives an immediate tax deduction but may spread out grants over future years. That works great if you need tax relief now but prefer to spread your charitable impact over a period of years. On the downside, donor-advised funds don't offer the same level of control as private foundations. It is unlikely but possible that the fund won't honor a donor's grant request. Donor-advised funds may not be able to accept certain illiquid assets that a private foundation would, like artwork and real estate.

If you wish to leave gifts to both charitable organizations and individuals (family, friends, etc.) after your death, consider how these assets are taxed before you decide which assets to give to charity. Some assets, like life insurance, are tax free to your heirs. Others, like retirement plans funded with pre-tax contributions, will create taxable income in respect of decedent (IRD). When choosing which assets to give to charity, remember that the charity will not have to pay taxes if they're using the IRD assets for their charitable purpose.

COGNITIVE DECLINE & DEATH

The National Institutes of Health estimate that one in seven Americans age 71 and older have dementia (https://www.nih.gov/news-events/news-releases/one-seven-americans-age-71-older-has-some-type-dementia-nih-funded-study-estimates). Concerns about cognitive function aren't exclusive to those already at retirement age, however. According to the Center for Disease Control, 10.8% of adults between the ages of 45-64 experience subjective cognitive decline, the self-reported experience of worsening or more frequent confusion or memory loss (https://www.cdc.gov/aging/aginginfo/subjective-cognitive-decline-brief.html).

Cognitive decline isn't pleasant to think about, but it is a fate that awaits many of us. Can you do anything to prevent this from happening to you? Can you at least make this situation manageable should it happen to you in the future? There are a few things that may help. Having open conversations with your doctor and qualified health professionals who understand your medical background is a great place to start. Presumably, they should be up to date on the latest research findings and be able to advise you on what preventative techniques and options are appropriate for you.

The mind and body are connected, so staying active and eating well should improve your odds of staying mentally fit. Subjective cognitive decline is less frequently reported by those with more years of formal education. Activities like reading, learning, and involving yourself in your community should help.

The blunt truth, however, is that dementia or cognitive decline may happen to you even if you do everything right. If you were to experience significant cognitive decline right now, are your affairs organized in such a way that you would be confident explaining them to someone in your inner circle? This is why planning and having an inner circle you trust is so important. If a plan is in motion, if people you trust understand your wishes and intentions, you may be able to face cognitive decline with grace, dignity, and equanimity. A complex plan can fall apart easily if not executed properly. Steps you've taken earlier in your retirement journey-choosing your inner circle, managing risks, estate planning, etc. - will make executing your plans simpler in the future.

LEADERSHIP & LEGACY

The world is a confusing place, and people are looking for inspiration and guidance. Who out there is looking to you for this? The knowledge that what we do matters to others should motivate us to set a good example. Some of us feel a greater natural sense of leadership than others. Not everyone feels like a leader or even wants to feel like a leader. Even if it feels like no one is paying attention, your words and actions carry weight. If it is within your power, be a source of wisdom and inspiration in this world, even if only for a moment. With awareness of the power of these moments, maybe their frequency and duration will grow and improve the lives of those around you.

If you do great things for yourself, will others really be inspired? Dr. Robert Cialdini, a psychologist renowned for his work on the subjects of influence and persuasion, identifies social proof as one of his 6 "weapons of influence" along with reciprocity, consistency, likability, authority, and scarcity. Social proof is the idea that in any given situation, behavior is viewed as more correct if we see other people doing it. This is a mental shortcut people use to know how to act in a variety of settings. Examples might include how much space people give each other in a restaurant, what topics are appropriate to joke about at a business networking meeting, or what styles of clothing are fashionable in a particular city. In a grander sense, social proof works to highlight the qualities we desire to see in others. For better or worse, your actions contribute to the social proof of a given behavior. How you discuss money and how you plan for your financial future may be modeled by others who respect your decision making. Social evidence can be more powerful than physical evidence.

As we established at the outset of this book, the structure of your retirement journey was derived from the concept of the Hero's Journey template used by storytellers throughout history. In the final stage of the Hero's Journey, the hero returns home to share the spoils of their victories. What is it that you wish to share? My hope for you is not only that you achieve victory, but that you are able to pass victory on. Victory can be many things, like money, knowledge, or love.

When your journey reaches its end, what legacy do you wish to leave behind? Seize the opportunity to shape it while you still can. Although our names will be forgotten a few generations from now, the consequences of our actions will continue to be felt by our inheritors. Our actions and our legacy are deeply intertwined. Legacy is grander than a plaque on a wall or a dollar figure on an investment account. Upon closer inspection, our legacy is the values, beliefs, and habits that future generations will inherit from us. To paraphrase Sir Isaac Newton, for every action we take in life, there is an equal and opposite reaction from an opposing force. As our energy interacts with these opposing forces, our legacy is embedded in the chain of events yet to unfold. Long after we're gone, the journey lives on.

POSTSCRIPT

Thank you for reading Financial Planning & You. I hope this book has given you some actionable ideas to help you move forward on your journey. There are valuable insights and strategies contained in these pages, but please remember that one book alone cannot be relied upon for personalized financial advice. Due to factors that are unique to all of our lives, a book can never replace the experience of working with a qualified financial advisor.

As you contemplate what you've read, ask yourself this question: What are ideas worth without actions? Take the right actions to accomplish your goals!

If you are ready to speak with an advisor like me about your retirement journey, please visit the Financial Planning & You website where you can reach out to me and say hello. My direct email address a.albidress@lpl.com. I look forward to answering your questions and hearing your feedback. The more I learn from you, the more I can serve my community.

Thanks again and I wish you success on your journey!

-Adrian Albidress, Jr. CFP® CPA

www.financialplanningandyou.com
www.albidressfinancial.com